Leckie✗Leckie
Scotland's leading educational publishers

Succe

HIGHER
Modern Studies

**Gemma McGrattan, Ruairidh Nicolson,
Derick Proctor & Anthony Rodgers**

Contents

Political issues in the United Kingdom

Devolved decision making in Scotland

Decision making in central government

Electoral systems, voting and political attitudes

Social issues in the United Kingdom

Wealth and health inequalities in the UK

International issues

Republic of South Africa

International issues

The People's Republic of China

The United States of America

Icons and features

Top Tips

Scotland and devolution

To prepare for the exam you should know about the following:
- The founding principles of the Scottish Parliament.
- The devolved and reserved matters and the areas where they overlap.
- The Additional Member System; the arguments for and against its use and its impact on the Scottish Parliament.
- The Scottish Government – advantages and disadvantages of coalition and minority government.
- The work of the Scottish Parliament, MSPs and the First Minister.
- Areas of conflict and co-operation between Holyrood and Westminster.
- Scottish local authorities – the services they provide, the way in which they are funded and conflict with the Scottish Government.
- The Single Transferable Vote electoral system used to elect councillors and the impact it has had.

Background information

'There shall be a Scottish Parliament.' (Donald Dewar speaking at the opening of the Scottish Parliament on 1 July 1999, quoting from the first section of the Scotland Act 1988.)

Donald Dewar is often seen as being the father of devolution.

Donald Dewar

When Labour came to power in 1997, a Bill was introduced into the UK Parliament in London which proposed that Scotland should have its own parliament. The Prime Minister at the time, Tony Blair, saw the creation of a Scottish Parliament as a step in tackling the 'democratic deficit' which had existed under the previous Conservative Governments. Scotland had consistently voted against the Conservatives – yet still ended up with a Conservative Government. Blair believed a Scottish Parliament would strengthen the UK and quell Scottish nationalism. Donald Dewar headed a Consultative Steering Group (CSG) to oversee the creation of the Scottish Parliament.

The Scottish Parliament is based on **four founding principles**:
- **Sharing power** – the Scottish Parliament should embody and reflect the sharing of power between the people of Scotland, the legislators (lawmakers) and the Scottish Government.
- **Accountability** – the Scottish Government must be accountable to the Scottish Parliament and the Scottish Parliament and Scottish Government should be accountable to the people of Scotland.
- **Equal opportunities** – the Scottish Parliament should be accessible and open to all. It should be responsive, and develop procedures which make possible a participative approach to the development, consideration and scrutiny of policy and legislation.
- **Accessibility** – the Scottish Parliament, in its operation and its appointments, should recognise the need to promote equal opportunities for all.

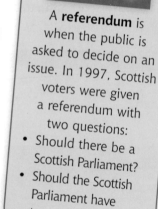
Scottish Parliament building under construction

A **referendum** was held on 11 September 1997. The people of Scotland voted in favour of the creation of a Scottish Parliament with tax-varying power. At the time of writing, this power had not been implemented, partly due to the cost of changing the taxation system. In 1998, the Scotland Act was passed by the UK Government – this enabled the creation of the Scottish Parliament and the beginning of devolution.

Devolution

Devolution is where a central government passes limited powers to a regional government. In this case, the UK Parliament passed powers to the Scottish Parliament. These powers are known as **devolved powers**. Some powers are reserved to the UK Parliament because Scotland is not an independent state (country). This ensures that, for example, borders are protected the same way all around the UK.

Devolved and reserved powers

Scotland has many devolved powers. On devolved matters, i.e. the areas that Scotland controls, the Scottish Parliament passes legislation (laws). As of June 2011, devolved matters include:

*   health
*   education and training
*   local government
*   social work
*   housing
*   planning
*   tourism, economic development and financial assistance to industry
*   some aspects of transport, including the Scottish road network, bus policy and ports and harbours
*   law and home affairs, including most aspects of criminal and civil law, the prosecution system and the courts
*   the Police and Fire services
*   the environment
*   natural and built heritage
*   agriculture, forestry and fishing
*   sport and the arts
*   statistics, public registers and records

(Source: http://www.scotland.gov.uk/About/18060/11552,)

The UK Government in London still retains some powers; these are called **reserved powers**. The major reserved powers include:

*   The constitution
*   Defence and national security
*   Foreign policy
*   Protection of borders
*   UK fiscal and monetary policy (other than Scotland's tax-varying power)
*   Employment law
*   Social security
*   Broadcasting
*   Transport and safety regulation – airports and motorways
*   Regulation of certain professions such as medicine and dentistry
*   Nuclear safety

Quick Test 1

1. What are the founding principles of the Scottish Parliament?
2. What is devolution?
3. Why are some powers reserved to the UK Parliament?

The electoral system of the Scottish Parliament – the Additional Member System

The electoral system used to elect Members of the Scottish Parliament (MSPs) is called the Additional Member System (AMS). It is a form of proportional representation which combines two voting systems, a vote by First Past The Post (FPTP) and a vote through the Party List system. It is the list system which brings an element of proportionality to the electoral system for the Scottish Parliament.

Under AMS, in Scottish Parliament elections, each voter has two votes:
- a regional vote
- a constituency vote.

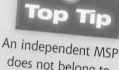

Ballot papers

The regional vote is used to elect 56 regional MSPs. Voters vote for a political party and each political party has a party list of candidates. The political parties decide in which order their candidates appear on their own party's list. Regional seats are **allocated proportionally** according to the number of votes cast for each party and individual candidates across the region, and the number of constituency seats won by each party in the region. Despite 'Alex Salmond for First Minister' appearing on ballot papers in both 2007 and 2011, voters do not elect the First Minister. The First Minister is elected by MSPs. After the 2011 election, Alex Salmond was elected by MSPs unopposed.

The MSPs elected via AMS are elected at a regional level to ensure that, as far as possible, the share of MSPs in the Scottish Parliament reflects the share of votes cast for each party within each electoral region. The eight electoral regions for the Scottish Parliament are:
- Highlands and Islands
- North East Scotland
- Mid Scotland and Fife
- West of Scotland
- Glasgow
- Central Scotland
- Lothians
- South of Scotland

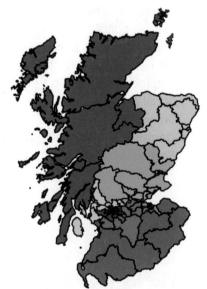

Scottish regions and constituencies

The constituency vote is used to elect the 73 constituency MSPs using the First Past The Post (FPTP) system. Each elector votes for a candidate in the constituency where he or she lives. Accordingly, 73 MSPs are elected to the Scottish Parliament via FPTP to represent individual constituencies. Each person in Scotland is represented by eight MSPs – one constituency MSP and seven MSPs for their region.

Impact of AMS on the Scottish Parliament

When setting up the Scottish Parliament in 1997, it was felt that FPTP would give the Labour Party an automatic outright majority; therefore a proportional system was needed to ensure a suitable and fully representative government was elected.

Due to the proportional nature of AMS, the impact it has had on the Scottish Parliament is that the political parties elected to government have to co-operate with opposition parties and opposition parties can more easily hold the government to account. It has allowed smaller political parties, such as the Green Party, a chance to have their views heard and to hold positions of power. This has helped to meet two of the founding principles of the Scottish Parliament, sharing power and accountability. However, in the May 2011 election, the SNP gained an overall majority.

Arguments used in support of AMS

- It is broadly proportional; the percentage of votes a party gets closely reflects the percentage of seats they get in parliament.
- Each voter has a directly accountable single constituency MSP.
- No wasted votes, every voter has at least one effective vote – voters can 'split their tickets'.
- Smaller parties get a better chance of having their views heard and being represented.

Arguments used against AMS

- Two different types of MSP are created, constituency MSPs and regional MSPs, each with different roles; this can be confusing for constituents.
- Political parties may have too much power; they decide who is on, and the order of, their party lists.
- AMS is likely to result in coalition or minority government, which could be seen as unrepresentative or weak government (because no-one actually votes for coalitions).
- Some people get confused by the fact they have two votes – at the 2007 election there were 140 000 invalid ballot papers due to confusion among the electorate and vote-counting machines malfunctioning.

Top Tip

AMS has helped smaller parties, such as the Green Party, get greater access to power in Parliament. After winning two seats in the 2007 election, the Greens entered into a co-operation agreement with the SNP. The SNP nominated the Green MSP Patrick Harvie Convenor of the Transport, Infrastructure and Climate Change committee in return for support of some SNP policies.

Quick Test 2

1. Explain the way in which the Additional Member System works.
2. What are the arguments for and against using AMS?

The Scottish Government

Scottish Parliament elections are usually held every four years. (The 2011 session will run until 2016 – five years.) The party with the most MSPs forms the Government. The Government is headed by the **First Minister** (the leader of the party forming the government). The First Minister chooses which MSPs will be in the Cabinet.

The Lab/Lib Coalition Governments 1999–2003, 2003–2007

The first parliamentary session ran from 1999 to 2003 and the Scottish Parliament's **first government was a coalition government** between the Labour Party and the Liberal Democrats.

A coalition is where two or more parties join together so they can govern as a majority. In order to form a coalition, parties must negotiate on some policies. After the 1999 election, Labour agreed to the Liberal Democrat policy of free personal care for the elderly. In 2003, the Liberal Democrats again made demands. They were successful in ensuring proportional representation was introduced to local council elections. Both of these policies were beneficial to the Liberal Democrats.

Donald Dewar,
(First Minister
1999–2000)

Advantages and disadvantages of coalition government

The political viewpoints of more voters are represented under a coalition than under a single party minority government. In a coalition, the parties forming a government have to **compromise on policies** – yet **no voter ever votes for compromise policies**. Because they have to compromise on policy issues and find common ground, coalition governments can be volatile. An example of this was the **free personal care compromise** between Scottish Labour and the Liberal Democrats.

Henry McLeish,
(First Minister
2000–2001)

When a large party is trying to form a coalition, a small party (or parties) with very few elected representatives can find itself in a position of great importance. This is excellent for that particular party and its voters. When a small party is placed in this position, it is known as the **'kingmaker'** as it holds the balance of power.

Jack McConnell
(First Minister
2001–2007)

Top Tip

Because the Additional Member System (AMS) is a form of proportional representation, the Scottish Parliament elections are likely to produce minority or coalition governments.

The SNP Minority Government 2007–2011

Alex Salmond (First Minister 2007–2011 remained FM after 2011 election)

In 2007, **the SNP formed the Scottish Parliament's first minority government**. In total, 129 Members of the Scottish Parliament were elected. In 2007 the SNP had 47 MSPs, Labour 46, Conservatives 17, Liberal Democrats 16, the Green Party 2, and there was 1 independent MSP. As the SNP had the largest number of MSPs elected, it formed the Government.

The SNP fell well short of the 65 MSPs needed to form a majority so they ruled as a minority government. The party relied on the support of other parties to pass laws.

Advantages of minority governments, such as in 2007–11

* **A minority government must co-operate with other political parties** to ensure that legislation is passed.
* A **minority government is well scrutinised** by opposition parties and the electorate.

Disadvantages of a minority government

* It is **difficult to pass policies**. In 2007, the SNP only had 47 MSPs, fewer than half of the seats in Parliament, and therefore had to rely on support from opposition parties to pass legislation.
* **Weak government**. Some key election pledges may be unable to be delivered without compromising. For example, the 2007–11 minority government could not cancel the Edinburgh tram project.
* **Opposition parties can stall progress and policies to make the minority government look weak**.

The SNP Majority Government, elected 2011

SNP Cabinet, 2011

On 5 May 2011, the SNP won 69 seats in the Scottish Parliament election, giving it an overall majority. The Liberal Democrat vote fell significantly and the SNP benefited from this. Labour emerged with 37 seats, while the Conservatives won 15. The Liberal Democrats won 5 seats while the Greens, as in 2007, secured 2 seats. Margo MacDonald was again returned to the Scottish Parliament as the only independent MSP.

Advantages of majority governments

* **Legislation can be passed quickly.**
* Majority governments have **strong mandates to govern**.

Disadvantages of majority governments

* There are **few checks on the power of majority governments**.
* **Conflict with Westminster**. Some opponents of the SNP believe that the party is too focused on securing independence and not focused enough on issues such as the economy and jobs.
* **The Scottish Parliament is a unicameral legislature**. This means it only has one component, unlike the UK Parliament, which has the House of Commons and the House of Lords. It was envisaged that the AMS system would prevent any party from securing an outright majority. The committee system, which was designed to scrutinise and revise legislation, has been severely weakened. Every committee has a significant presence of SNP MSPs who can influence decision making.

Quick Test 3

1. Describe the advantages and disadvantages of a coalition government.
2. Discuss the arguments for and against the view that a minority government is better than a coalition.

The work of the Scottish Parliament, MSPs and the First Minister

Powers of the First Minister (FM)

Leader of the majority

The FM is elected by the Scottish Parliament's 129 MSPs. The **FM can steer the agenda** as he or she has the **democratic mandate**. Because the First Minister has this mandate, he or she is seen as the most **important figure** in the eyes of voters and media alike. As a result of the 2011 election, the SNP First Minister Alex Salmond holds a great deal of power, especially since the SNP has an overall majority of MSPs.

Relationship with the other parts of the UK and foreign dignitaries

The First Minister can **assist Ministers of the Crown**. Former Labour FM Jack McConnell set up aid funds to help Malawi – this was done despite the UK having a department to assist with overseas development (DFID). The First Minister can **lead delegations** abroad and **meet with foreign dignitaries** when they visit Scotland. The First Minister **represents the interests of Scotland at meetings with UK Government ministers**.

Power of patronage

Many MSPs are career-minded and would like to hold positions of power within the Scottish Government. It is the **First Minister who decides which MSP leads each Government department**. This gives the First Minister power over the MSPs in his or her party. If MSPs do not agree with the Government, they can quickly find themselves out of favour with the First Minister and their chances of promotion fading.

The Government is held to account by the opposition MSPs. The following are the main ways in which the Government is held to account:

First Minister's Question Time

First Minister's Question Time (FMQs) is held every Thursday in the debating chamber of the Scottish Parliament. It is an opportunity for MSPs to hold the Scottish Government to account and to raise pressing issues with the First Minister. MSPs who wish to question the First Minister must submit their questions prior to FMQs. Questions are then selected by the Presiding Officer.

The format of FMQs means preference is given to opposition party leaders. The leader of the largest opposition party asks the first question, with the other party leaders asking their questions thereafter. FMQs can be very confrontational. The questions tend to be topical – MSPs usually ask questions about issues which are currently in the media spotlight and/or about the concerns of their constituents. To get a grasp on the current issues, it's a good idea to watch FMQs online. It can be viewed online on catch-up services.

The work of MSPs

MSPs are elected to represent their constituents. MSPs work in the Scottish Parliament on Tuesdays, Wednesdays and Thursdays. When they are not in parliament, they devote their time to meeting constituents at regular surgeries and public events, and to attending meetings. MSPs can represent their constituents in the Scottish Parliament in the ways outlined below.

Parliamentary written and oral questions

MSPs can put **written questions to Scottish Ministers**. These questions often relate to **the concerns of constituents**. MSPs expect responses from the relevant Ministers. The responses are usually drafted by civil servants and then signed by the appropriate Government Minister. For example, if an MSP submits a written question about the Curriculum for Excellence, he or she would expect a response from the Cabinet Secretary for Education and Lifelong Learning. The database of written questions can be accessed at: www.scottish. parliament.uk/ and following the Parliamentary Business > Motions, Questions and answer links. It's a good idea to have a look on this database to find some questions which your MSPs have asked. The database is updated regularly and you will find up-to-date information to use as examples in the exam.

MSPs can hold the Government to account during **debates on specific issues**. As well as putting forward questions for consideration at FMQs, MSPs can ask questions during Question Time debates. Question Time in the Scottish Parliament can be themed, general or about single specific issues. For example, there was a debate on a Scottish Government Motion to treat the Offensive Behaviour at Football and Threatening Communications (Scotland) Bill as an Emergency Bill in June 2011. Debates in the Scottish Parliament give MSPs more opportunities to hold the Scottish Government to account. MSPs can also propose motions to be debated in the chamber. These debates can stimulate responses from other MSPs, the media and the public.

Making laws

The Scottish Parliament building

There are many opportunities for MSPs to take part in the law-making process. When a proposal for a new law is introduced to the Parliament, it is known as a **Bill**. Bills must be **debated** and **voted on** through **three stages** before they can become law. MSPs can even propose new laws and introduce Members' Bills into the Parliament. A good example of a Member's Bill is Margo MacDonald's **End of Life Assistance (Scotland) Bill** of 2010. This Bill was debated by parliament but did not become a law.

You can read more about the law-making process at www.scottish.parliament.uk/parliamentarybusiness/Bills.aspx

Voting

Voting in the Scottish Parliament is very high tech. MSPs use their ID cards to activate electronic voting machines located at each seat. In the third session of the Scottish Parliament, which ran from 2007–11, the SNP had to rely on the opposition parties for support in order to pass bills through each stage. For example, the SNP relied on the Scottish Conservatives to pass their budget each year. However, since the election on 5 May 2011, the SNP has had an overall majority of MSPs and so no longer has to rely on the support of opposition MSPs to pass Bills through the Scottish Parliament.

Committees

During the creation of the Scottish Parliament and the devolved settlement, it was agreed that the Scottish Parliament would have a strong committee system. Scottish Parliament committees are small groups of MSPs who focus on specific areas. **Committees are very important to the work of the Scottish Parliament.**

Some committees, such as the **Finance Committee**, are **mandatory**. As well as mandatory committees, **Subject Committees** are established at the beginning of each parliamentary session. At the time of writing, Subject Committees included the **Health and Sport Committee** and the **Justice Committee**. Up-to-date information on committees and members can be found at: www.scottish.parliament.uk/ and following the Parliamentary Business > Committees links.

As well as mandatory and subject committees, Private Bill and other committees can also be formed. For example, there have been committees on the Edinburgh Tram Bill, the Glasgow Airport Rail Link Bill, and the End of Life Assistance (Scotland) Bill.

MSPs can use committees to put forward the views of their constituents. Each committee of the Scottish Parliament is made up of MSPs from different political parties. **They have a great deal of power**, including:

The ability to call witnesses and oblige Cabinet Secretaries (and civil servants) to attend. They can even call the First Minister to give evidence.
The ability to hold inquiries.
The ability to initiate legislation – committees can propose new laws.

The **Public Petitions Committee** considers all petitions put to it. It is very accessible and petitions can be created online.

Some Scottish Parliament committees have met in different venues around Scotland – sometimes in places far from Edinburgh. Usually members of the public can sit in and listen to the proceedings of committees – though they are not allowed to participate.

Cross-party groups

MSPs can form **Cross-party groups (CPGs)**. CPGs act as forums for MSPs of all parties, external organisations and members of the public to meet and discuss issues about which they feel strongly. An example of a CPG in the 2007–11 session of the Scottish Parliament was the **Crofting Cross Party Group**. Members of this CPG included some Highland and Islands MSPs.

The Work of MSPs

MSPs are elected to represent their constituents. MSPs work in the Scottish Parliament on Tuesdays, Wednesdays and Thursdays. When they are not in parliament, they devote their time to meeting constituents at regular surgeries and public events, and to attending meetings. Surgeries are sessions where constituents can meet with MSPs to raise issues and discuss concerns. MSPs often hold joint surgeries with councillors of the same party.

The following extract from an MSP's diary shows how busy they can be.

24 January 2011 – 30 January 2011	
24 Monday	**25 Tuesday**
09:30–10:30 Staff meeting (Inverness) 12:30–14:30 Lunch with Provost 19:30–21:00 Surgery (Elgin Community Centre)	Travel to Edinburgh 13:00–14:00 Whips meeting 14:45–15:30 Health Team 18:00–19:30 Women's Aid reception
26 Wednesday	**27 Thursday**
09:15–09:45 Phone conference 10:00–12:00 Health Committee 13:00–14:15 Labour Group (Room M1.2) 14:00–15:00 Stage 3 Debate 17:00 18:00–19:30 Marie Curie reception	09:30–10:30 Chamber Duty 11:20–12:00 General Questions 12:00–12:30 FMQ 14:15–15:00 Budget Statement 15:00–17:00 Budget Debate 17:00 Decision Time
28 Friday	**29 Saturday**
10:30–12:00 Campaign Meeting (Glasgow) 17:30–21:00 Unison Meeting (Inverness)	11:00–13:00 Surgery (Caol Community Centre)
30 Sunday	

Quick Test 4

1. In what ways can an MSP represent constituents in the Scottish Parliament?
2. Why is the committee system important to the work of the Scottish Parliament?

Areas of conflict and co-operation between Holyrood and Westminster

Areas of co-operation

While politicians from Holyrood and Westminster may argue over many issues, in practice there is a great deal of co-operation between the civil servants of both governments. The UK Government is still the sovereign government. With consent from the Scottish Parliament, Westminster can pass laws which apply to Scotland – even if these areas are devolved. In certain circumstances it can be sensible and advantageous for Scotland if, with the consent of the Scottish Parliament (signified by approval of an appropriate motion), Scottish Ministers agree with the UK Government that a Westminster Bill should include provisions on devolved matters. Scottish Ministers will consider promoting a **Legislative Consent Motion** (previously known as a 'Sewel Motion') in a number of circumstances:

- Where it would be more effective to legislate on a UK basis in order to put in place a single UK-wide regime (e.g. powers for the courts to confiscate the assets of serious offenders).
- Where there is a complex inter-relationship between reserved and devolved matters that can most effectively and efficiently be dealt with in a single Westminster Bill (e.g. the introduction of civil partnerships).
- Where the UK Parliament is considering legislation for England and Wales which the Scottish Government believes should also be brought into effect in Scotland, but no parliamentary time is available at Holyrood (e.g. to strengthen protection against sex offenders).
- Where the provisions in question, although they relate to devolved matters, are minor or technical and uncontroversial (e.g. powers for Scottish Ministers to vary the functions of the Central Council for Education and Training in Social Work).

Scottish Ministers can also provide support to UK Government ministers. This happened under the leadership of former Labour First Minister Jack McConnell. McConnell felt it would be appropriate for the Scottish Government to give aid to Malawi. While viewed as being admirable and positive by many, the Scottish Government was replicating the work of the UK's Department for International Development. However, both the Scottish Parliament's and Westminster's work on this issue continued.

Areas of conflict

Justice

The SNP has called for the Scottish Parliament to have powers surrounding the **use of air guns** devolved. This issue gained momentum in 2005 following the case of Mark Bonini, who was found guilty of murdering two-year-old Andrew Morton in the Easterhouse area of Glasgow. Bonini shot the toddler in the head with an air rifle. The SNP sees the use of air guns in crimes as a particularly Scottish problem.

Foreign affairs

The **war in Iraq** was debated by MSPs, and the Scottish Parliament voted on the issue, despite the case for UK armed forces being deployed being a reserved issue. Many MSPs made the point that Scottish troops would be involved.

The high-profile case of **Abdelbaset Mohmed Ali al-Megrahi** – the Lockerbie bomber – proved problematic. Megrahi had been found guilty under Scots law and had been sentenced for planting a bomb on Pan Am flight 103 in 1988. The bomb went off in UK airspace and the wreckage of the flight landed in a Scottish town called Lockerbie. Megrahi received a life sentence and was serving the sentence in Barlinnie jail in Scotland. After he was diagnosed with incurable prostate cancer in 2009, Scotland's Justice Secretary Kenny MacAskill MSP decided to release Megrahi on compassionate grounds. This provoked a furious reaction from politicians in the USA who did not want Megrahi released and the leader of the UK Conservative Party, David Cameron publicly announced he thought that Kenny MacAskill made the wrong decision. While Justice is a devolved issue, the fallout of the situation left the UK Government (which still has foreign affairs under its control) blaming the Scottish Government. This is a good example of overlap between devolved and reserved powers.

Abdelbaset al-Megrahi

Immigration

Scotland's population has been stagnating and the average age of the population has been increasing. In order to increase the number of people moving to Scotland, **the Lab/Lib Government introduced a Fresh Talent initiative in 2004**, which encouraged people to consider coming to live and work in Scotland. It also tried to encourage recent graduates from Scottish universities to remain in Scotland. Since immigration was a matter that was reserved to the UK Government, agreement had to be obtained from the Home Office so that non-European-Union graduates from Scottish universities could stay on for two years following graduation to seek employment. Opposition towards the scheme was voiced by some English universities which felt that the initiative gave Scottish universities a competitive advantage in terms of attracting students from overseas. The Fresh Talent Initiative ended on 29 June 2008 when the UK Government brought in a new points-based immigration scheme.

Top Tip

The Scottish Parliament and UK Parliament have experienced both co-operation and conflict. Co-operation can be highlighted by the use of Legislative Consent Motions and conflict can be seen in areas such as education (university tuition fees) and immigration (treatment of asylum seeker families living in Scotland).

Dawn raids

There was also conflict between Holyrood and Westminster over the **removal of asylum seekers** who had failed to gain the right to remain in the UK. Glasgow City Council housed a significant number of asylum seekers and the UK Home Office employed a strategy of 'dawn raids' on the homes of *failed* asylum seekers. These people were held in the Dungavel Detention Centre (located in South Lanarkshire) with their children. Since social work and education are devolved issues, MSPs campaigned for the rights of the asylum seeker's children and for the Scottish Government to be given control over the removal of failed asylum seekers. The Westminster Coalition Government has ceased using Dungavel and now asylum seekers with failed right-to-remain applications are held in detention centres in England before being sent back to their countries of origin. Criticism of this new arrangement exists – failed asylum seekers who are moved to detention centres in England find themselves further away from their lawyers.

Education

While student top-up fees were introduced in England, with the support of Labour MPs who represented Scottish constituencies, student tuition fees were abolished in Scotland by the Scottish Parliament.

UK/Scottish Government relations

The West Lothian Question

Prior to the devolution referendum in 1979, the Labour Member of Parliament for West Lothian, Tam Dalyell, expressed concerns. Dalyell was worried that, with the creation of a Scottish Parliament, Scottish MPs at Westminster would lose influence and power over issues which would affect their constituencies (the constituency being the area and people they represent). Dalyell saw **devolution** as being the **motorway to independence, with no exits**.

The concerns which he expressed at the time have not emerged since the creation of the Scottish Parliament. The situation has been quite different. Scottish MPs at Westminster were actually relied upon to pass legislation on the creation of foundation hospitals and also student top-up fees. **Scottish MPs voting on laws which only affected England was seen as being very unfair by many people.**

Over-representation

Many people argue that Scotland is still over-represented at Westminster. A condition of the Scotland Act 1998 was to oversee the number of Scottish MPs being returned to Westminster reduced. **The number fell from 72 to its current level – 59.** The current Prime Minister, David Cameron, **would like to see the current number of Scottish MPs cut further**. At the time of writing, there have been no proposals to carry out this reduction.

The Calman Commission and the National Conversation

The Calman Commission

The Calman Commission was backed by the main political parties, with the exception of the SNP. Headed by Sir Kenneth Calman, the Commission was tasked:

> *To review the provisions of the Scotland Act 1998 in the light of experience and to recommend any changes to the present constitutional arrangements that would enable the Scottish Parliament to serve the people of Scotland better, improve the financial accountability of the Scottish Parliament, and continue to secure the position of Scotland within the United Kingdom.*

Top Tip

The Calman Commission was created to make devolution work more effectively and to strengthen the Union.

Published in 2009, the key recommendations of the Calman Report include:
* The transfer of powers to Scotland surrounding **air weapons**.
* Scotland being given **control over drink-drive limits**. (The current limit is higher in the UK than the rest of continental Europe.)
* Holyrood being given the power to change **speed limits** on roads.
* **The Scottish Parliament being given control over Scottish elections**. This is a very sensitive point after the 2007 Scottish parliamentary elections were besieged with problems, including votes being rejected by counting machines. (Estimates of 140 000 votes not being counted correctly led to a public outcry.)

- **A 10p cut in all income tax rates in Scotland**, with a corresponding reduction in the annual block grant from the Treasury. There have been calls for Scotland to raise its own taxes and therefore increase accountability in spending – the Scottish Parliament would have to levy part or all of the 10p rate.
- Holyrood to be given **additional borrowing powers for capital expenditure**. This would enable the Scottish Government to borrow money to pay for major projects like the construction of a new bridge over the Firth of Forth.
- The current finance mechanism to remain in place until a new mechanism is developed.
- **Co-operation between Westminster and Holyrood to be strengthened**. Ministers from each legislature should appear before relevant committees. The Commission recommended there be official channels of communication between UK and Scottish Government Ministers. At the time, the relationship between the SNP minority government at Holyrood and Labour at Westminster was strained.

However, the Calman Commission report not only recommended that Scotland be given more powers, but that some powers should be taken back by Westminster. The Commission recommended that powers of insolvency, charity law and registration of health professionals be returned to Westminster.

The National Conversation

Instead of backing the Calman Commission, First Minister Alex Salmond launched the 'National Conversation' in August 2007. The National Conversation consulted widely, with members of the public being able to express their views on its website. The National Conversation explored devolving powers further and, unlike the Calman Commission, explored Scottish independence. At the time of writing, the Scotland Bill 2010–11 was being considered by the House of Lords in London. The Bill is being considered in order to implement the recommendations of the Calman Report. There are aspects of the Bill that the SNP does not agree with.

However, the Bill (in its current form) would see changes to Scotland's finances, including a new Scottish rate of income tax. Though the SNP supports some points in the Bill, it is against other parts. The SNP believes that income tax proposals in the Scotland Bill have flaws and would leave Scotland worse off. It is also opposed to the decision to return some devolved powers to Westminster.

Supreme Court

Almost immediately after the 2011 election, senior Scottish Ministers found themselves embroiled in a war of words with the UK Supreme Court over a number of issues. With Justice being a devolved issue, Scottish Ministers faced a situation where cases were being reviewed by the Supreme Court. In one instance, this led to the quashing of a conviction. At the time of writing, this issue had not been resolved and the conflict was continuing. On constitutional issues, it is envisaged that the UK Supreme Court could have a great deal of power if a referendum on Scotland becoming independent is called in the future.

Quick Test 5

1. To what extent do the Scottish Parliament and UK Parliament work in co-operation?
2. Describe what the Calman Commission is and give some of its key recommendations.

Funding for Scotland and the Barnett Formula

Where does Scotland's funding come from?

Scotland receives its funding each year from the UK Government. The amount that Scotland receives is set by Westminster. The system used to calculate **changes** in funding for devolved areas is called the **Barnett Formula**. It was drawn up in 1978 as a temporary measure but remains in place to this day. While the Barnett Formula is used to calculate changes in the amount of money Scotland receives from the UK Treasury, this money is a 'Block Grant'. Holyrood can spend this money as it wishes and does **not** have to follow Westminster's allocations.

Money also comes into Scotland via non-devolved routes such as the military. This can have a big effect on local economies. For example, it is feared that the announced conversion of RAF Leuchars into an army base will negatively affect the economy in this part of the country.

The way money is allocated

For every £1 the Government distributes to England, Scotland and Wales, roughly 85p goes to England, 10p to Scotland and 5p to Wales. With 5 million people, Scotland now has only 8·3% of the UK population. **That has led to a situation where 'identifiable spending' in Scotland on public services is £1500 higher per person than in England**. (In 2009–10, UK Government spending on public services in England was £8559 per person, in Scotland £10083, in Wales £9587 and in Northern Ireland £10662. [Source: www.independent.co.uk/news/uk/politics/england-versus-scotland-a-crossborder-dispute-2306012.html]) While this difference was uncontroversial when it was agreed upon, it has become controversial in recent years.

The SNP Government views on funding

The SNP believes that Scotland should be independent and sees the money that Scotland receives from Westminster as 'pocket money'. Scotland does not have control over funding and does not raise its own taxes. As a consequence, major infrastructure projects such as a new Forth Road Bridge are problematic. The SNP argues that Scotland should be given the power to borrow money, while the Conservative/Liberal Democrat Government at Westminster argues that major projects should be undertaken from the funding that Scotland already receives.

UK Government position on the Barnett Formula

Prior to the UK Government's Comprehensive Spending Review of 2010, many people believed that George Osborne, the UK Chancellor, would abolish the Barnett Formula. However, this did not happen. Before becoming Prime Minister, David Cameron visited Edinburgh. During this visit he said **'better an imperfect marriage than a perfect divorce'**, publically stating that he does not want to see an end to the Union.

Many political commentators in Scotland believe that David Cameron does not want to be the Prime Minister who oversees the break-up of the UK.

Barnett Formula and spending in future

Top Tip

It costs more to deliver services such as healthcare, education and policing in Scotland than in England. This is because the population in Scotland is spread over a wider area.

Brian Taylor, the chief political editor of BBC Scotland, gave a lecture as part of the Edinburgh Lectures series. During his lecture, he pointed out that while the original system still operates, there has been **a narrowing of the gap in spending between Scotland and England**. However, spending per person in Scotland does remain higher and, since 1999, some policies have been introduced in Scotland which have not been introduced in England. Most notably, these include:

Free personal care for all elderly people in Scotland
The introduction of free eye tests
The abolition of prescription charges for all in Scotland – regardless of income.

While these have proved very popular, the Scottish Government may have to reconsider these policies due to spending being squeezed.

One measure already introduced is the merger of LTS and HMIE. The new body is called Education Scotland.

Case Study

In 2008, student tuition fees in Scotland were abolished by the minority SNP Government. The funding for this comes from the block grant. In England, the financial situation for students is very different. Student tuition fees in England were introduced by the previous Labour-led UK Government. This measure was supported by Scottish MPs. Today, prospective students in England face tuition fees of up to £9000 per year, depending on which institution they apply to.

There has been a great deal of debate regarding prospective students living in England applying to higher education institutions in Scotland. Prospective students living in England will have to pay fees if they attend Scottish higher education institutions, albeit perhaps at reduced rates. Prospective students living in Scotland will not have to pay fees to attend the same institutions.

Quick Test 6

1. Describe what the Barnett Formula is.
2. What concerns does the SNP have in regard to the current finance arrangements?

Local councils

Local councils in Scotland are sometimes referred to as local government or local authorities. In total, **there are 32 councils in Scotland**.

Edinburgh council

Just as Westminster has devolved certain powers to the Scottish Parliament, the Scottish Parliament has devolved powers to local councils. While the laws and decisions made at Holyrood are made by MSPs, decisions at local authorities are made by locally-elected councillors – they know the needs of their own areas. Local councillors represent people in their local wards by holding surgeries, attending council meetings and voting at council meetings.

Following the Lib/Lab coalition deal of 2003, the Single Transferable Vote (STV) system is now be used to elect councillors. Voters in Scotland are now required to list their preferences for their local councillors with number 1 being their first preference, number 2 being their second preference and so on. Councillors represent multi-member wards with three or four councillors representing each area. With the introduction of STV, Labour lost control of many councils across Scotland.

Some services councils provide are **mandatory** and some are **discretionary**.

The mandatory services which councils must legally provide include:
- Education
- Police
- Fire brigade
- Social work
- Sanitation

Discretionary services include:
- Swimming pools
- Gala days
- Town twinning
- Rural lighting
- Flood control

Council funding and spending

Councils receive funds in four ways:
- **Grants from the Scottish Government**.
  80% of the funding that Scotland's 32 councils receive comes in the form of these grants.
- **Council tax**.
  - In Scotland, properties were valued in 1993 for Council Tax purposes. Each property was placed into a 'valuation band'. The valuation band a property is in determines how much Council Tax must be paid. You can use www.saa.gov.uk to find out the bands properties fall into. If you input a postcode, this website will list the bands for the properties in that area.
  - Levels of Council Tax vary from council to council. To find out the levels of Council Tax in the authority in which you live, use an internet search engine.

Top Tip
Providing 'best value' – councils in Scotland must prove that they are sourcing the most cost-effective service.

- Council Tax is used towards paying for services. A large proportion of council spending goes on education and social work.
- **Fees** from libraries, swimming pool entrance costs and parking fines.
- **Private Public Partnerships (PPPs)**.
  - In PPPs, councils work with businesses to provide services and to build new accommodation, for example schools. The SNP Government is against PPP and created the Scottish Futures Trust (SFT) – a company owned by the Scottish Government. Set up in September 2008, the aim of the trust is to improve public infrastructure investment in the hope of saving £100–£150 million each year.

Co-operation and conflict between Scottish local councils and the Scottish Government

Cooperation

The Council of Scottish Local Authorities (COSLA) was created in 1975 to promote and protect the interests of councils in Scotland. COSLA gathers the views of Scottish councils and communicates these to the Scottish Government and the public. When the SNP came into power, a **concordat** was set out which established the terms of a new relationship between the Scottish Government and local government. This concordat was based on mutual respect and partnership, in that Local Authorities were given more control over how they allocated their budgets (ring-fencing was removed.) The new relationship was represented by a package of measures and was endorsed by both the Scottish Ministers and the COSLA presidential team. This concordat allows local authorities to retain all of their efficiency savings.

To prepare for the 2014 Commonwealth Games, there has been a great deal of cooperation between the Scottish Government and Glasgow City Council.

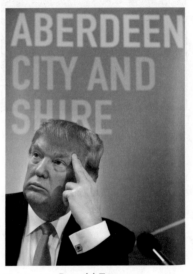

Donald Trump

Conflict

Conflict between the Scottish Government and Scotland's local authorities is nothing new. **When Jack McConnell was the First Minister (2001–2007), he declared a 'war on neds'**. McConnell looked at the use of Anti Social Behaviour Orders (ASBOs) to tackle youth crime in England. This led to conflict with councils. McConnell wanted to see more use of ASBOs but councils were reluctant due to the extra costs for social work departments and policing.

Prior to being elected in 2007, the SNP made an election promise of reducing class sizes. Councils were told to find the finances to do this. However, as well as having to find the funds to recruit teachers, councils found school accommodation unsuitable for delivering smaller class sizes.

The **SNP Government also froze council tax**. While this was a popular policy with voters, it deprived councils of revenue. Many Scottish local authorities would like to see the freeze end.

A further example of conflict was when US tycoon Donald Trump saw his application to build a golf course in Aberdeenshire turned down by Aberdeenshire Council. The Scottish Government intervened and overturned the council's decision. The golf course development went ahead and was opened in 2011.

Quick Test 7

1. Why was the Single Transferable Vote electoral system introduced to elect local councillors in Scotland?
2. Give examples of areas of conflict between local government and the Scottish Government.

The Executive

To prepare for the exam you should know about the following:
- The functions, powers, and composition of the Executive.
- The move towards Prime Ministerial government.
- The role of the Civil Service and tensions between the Civil Service and special advisors.
- The respective roles of Opposition and backbench MPs in holding the Executive to account.
- The role of the House of Lords in advising on legislation and the debate on House of Lords reform.
- The effectiveness of different types of pressure groups in influencing the legislative process.
- The impact of the media in influencing the decision making process and holding the Executive to account.

Background information

British governments are, in practice, formed by the leader of the party that wins the largest number of seats in the **House of Commons**. Until very recently, the winning party could nearly always count on having more than half of the seats in Parliament – thus forming a single party **majority government** – due to the **First Past The Post** (FPTP) electoral system. In the 2010 General Election, no party gained an overall majority of seats. A **Coalition Government** has therefore operated between the Conservatives and the Liberal Democrats.

David Cameron (right) had to answer embarrassing questions about past comments he had made about Nick Clegg (left) when they formed the Coalition Government in May 2010.

The **Executive** is the branch of Government that is concerned with policy and is led by the **Prime Minister** and **Cabinet**. The Cabinet is made up of **Ministers** who direct Government departments with the help of civil servants.

Ministers are usually MPs chosen from the Prime Minister's party. Under the current Coalition Government, there are MPs from both parties in the Cabinet.

It is the job of the Government to manage the economy, regulate business, handle public spending, conduct foreign policy and deal with a host of other matters.

Top Tip

When no party wins an overall majority the current Prime Minister is traditionally permitted to try to form a government first. Both Edward Heath in 1974 and Gordon Brown in 2010 faced this situation. Both failed to form governments. This situation is known as a **hung parliament**.

The Prime Minister (PM)

The Prime Minister is the head of the UK Government. In theory he or she is 'first among equals' in the Cabinet. The role of the Prime Minister has evolved, however, and continues to evolve. From 1979 onwards, Prime Minister Margaret Thatcher noticeably advanced the trend towards 'Presidential' government in which the PM plays a dominant rather than consensual role. In the absence of a formal written constitution laying down the duties and powers of the PM, holders of the office have been able to tailor the job to their own style and personality. However, the main duties of the PM can be summarised as follows:

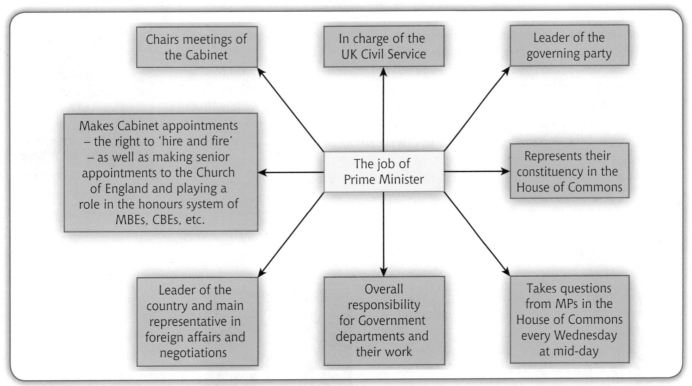

Chairs meetings of the Cabinet

In charge of the UK Civil Service

Leader of the governing party

Makes Cabinet appointments – the right to 'hire and fire' – as well as making senior appointments to the Church of England and playing a role in the honours system of MBEs, CBEs, etc.

The job of Prime Minister

Represents their constituency in the House of Commons

Leader of the country and main representative in foreign affairs and negotiations

Overall responsibility for Government departments and their work

Takes questions from MPs in the House of Commons every Wednesday at mid-day

Recent Prime Ministers

Tony Blair (Labour) 1997–2007
- Won major (landslide) victories at the 1997 and 2001 elections and a third victory in 2005 though with a smaller margin of victory.
- Delegated policy making decisions to special advisors and relied less on the Cabinet.
- Tumultuous relationship with Chancellor of the Exchequer Gordon Brown, who was given freedom of action in social and economic policy.
- Split Labour Party with controversial policies such as the Iraq war.
- Focused much of his time on foreign affairs and the 'war on terrorism' and had close relationship with US President George W. Bush.

Tony Blair

Gordon Brown (Labour) 2007–2010
- Took over from Blair as Labour leader and Prime Minister in 2007.
- Time in office rocked by economic crisis and recession.
- Seen as aloof and tribal by some ministerial colleagues, provoking resignations (e.g. Caroline Flint and James Purnell).
- Authority diminished by not having won his own **mandate** in an election and for missing opportunity to call one in October 2007.
- Negative public image and relentless criticism in media.
- Was accused of bullying and intimidation of junior staff.
- Defeated in 2010 General Election.

Gordon Brown

David Cameron (Conservative) 2010–present
- First Conservative Prime Minister since 1997.
- Power constrained by coalition agreement with the Liberal Democrats; has re-established position of Deputy Prime Minister for Lib Dem leader Nick Clegg.
- Far more emphasis on presentation than Gordon Brown; far closer to Tony Blair in that regard – once described himself as the 'heir to Blair'.
- Criticised for surrounding himself with private school and millionaire friends in Cabinet.
- Coalition agreement pledged to cut numbers of special advisors.

David Cameron

How powerful is the Prime Minister?

Despite moves towards 'Presidential' government, several factors continue to constrain the power of the Prime Minister:

James Purnell resigned from the Government in June 2009.

- General elections are now fixed on specific dates every five years and the PM must answer for the decisions of his or her government before the electorate. Margaret Thatcher and Gordon Brown were both felt by many Cabinet colleagues to have become an electoral liability.
- A Prime Minister also depends on the support of their MPs and Ministers. For example, in June 2009, James Purnell resigned from Gordon Brown's Cabinet and called for him to quit, but Brown survived the challenge. David Cameron faces the challenge of keeping both Conservative and Liberal Democrat MPs happy.
- Prime Ministers must sometimes include powerful enemies in the Cabinet to prevent them from causing the Government trouble from the backbenches. There were rumoured to be disagreements over policy between the modernising Conservative PM David Cameron and his Secretary of Defence, Liam Fox, who represents the values of many traditional Conservatives. However, Fox remained in the Cabinet until October 2011 when a personal scandal, rather than the Prime Minister, forced him out.
- A hostile media can weaken the authority of a Prime Minister. Gordon Brown was attacked by newspapers such as the *Daily Mail* and the *Sun* and had a consistently negative public image among large sections of the electorate (see section on the media on pages 34–35).

Top Tip

The role of the Prime Minister is different from that of the President of the United States, who is directly elected for a four-year term and will only have to resign if impeached for breaking the law. Prime Ministers and their governments can be brought down by one or a combination of the factors listed.

Bad press: Gordon Brown had a difficult time in the media.

The Cabinet

The Cabinet consists of a group of **Ministers** who manage Government departments. Ministers are appointed by the Prime Minister. Cabinet Ministers must be either a member of the **House of Commons** or the **House of Lords**. The Cabinet is where different departments, agendas, and even different beliefs and ideologies, meet to consider legislation and reach agreement. It is the job of the Prime Minister to chair meetings of the Cabinet, decide what it will discuss and sum up its mood after meetings. This potentially gives a PM a great deal of power over policy, although some Prime Ministers (e.g. Tony Blair) actually preferred to consult others for advice (see section on recent Prime Ministers). Once a decision is taken, each member of the Cabinet must support it. This is known as **collective responsibility**. Ministers must actually resign before publically criticising Cabinet decisions.

> **Top Tip**
>
> Ministers in charge of large Government departments are sometimes called Secretaries of State, for example the Secretary of State for Health. The term Minister and Secretary of State are used interchangeably.

Ministerial responsibility

Cabinet members must accept **ministerial responsibility**, which means that they are responsible for the work of their department. Mistakes, even by civil servants, can potentially lead to resignations of Ministers and Parliament will hold Ministers to account for their actions as heads of department.

> **Top Tip**
>
> Cabinets are regularly reshuffled and even names of departments can be changed. Keep up to date with the changing membership of the British Cabinet with the Cabinet Office website, www. cabinetoffice.gov.uk/ government-business/ government- ministers- responsibilities.aspx

In July 2010, Education Secretary Michael Gove announced a list of schools that would be rebuilt under a programme inherited from the previous Government. It later emerged that many of these schools would not be rebuilt at all. This resulted in criticism of Gove and he was forced to apologise to Parliament. He managed to keep his job. However, other Ministers have not been so lucky when something has gone wrong.

The work of the Cabinet is increasingly complex and, because it only has 25 members and usually only meets once a week, it cannot decide all matters of Government policy. A number of Cabinet committees have therefore been created to manage specific aspects of Government policy. One such Committee is the **National Security Council**, established by David Cameron in May 2010, which co-ordinates Government security and anti-terrorism policy.

The Civil Service

The Civil Service is the bureaucracy of the government. Civil servants are professionals who have permanent contracts: this means that they are in their posts long-term and, although political appointees and ministers will change depending on the party in power, Civil Service personnel will remain. The main aspects of the Civil Service's work are:

*   giving **policy advice to Ministers**. Senior civil servants advise Ministers how laws can and should be implemented.
*   Day-to-day staffing and **management of departments**.
*   **Implementing policy**. It is the job of the Civil Service to decide how laws passed by Parliament can be implemented in practice, which in theory gives them a great deal of power.
*   **Delivering services**. The staff of many front-line government services (e.g. Job Centres) are also civil servants.

The fact that civil servants actually implement Government policy means that they may have a great deal of expertise in their fields. There has sometimes been suspicion of civil servants running their own agendas in defiance of the wishes of Ministers. This has been embedded into popular consciousness by the BBC comedy *Yes, Minister*, where devious and cynical civil servants do their best to thwart the agenda of the elected (but incompetent) Minister.

Governments have indeed been concerned about being thwarted by civil cervants when trying to implement radical policy. Some left-wing critics see the Civil Service as an Oxbridge educated elite which will always favour the Conservatives, while civil servants are sometimes accused by Conservatives of being reluctant to consider public sector cuts or private sector solutions.

The fact that civil servants are always in their posts, no matter what political party is in power, means that they must be **politically neutral**. In other words, they cannot take sides or seek to obstruct the policies of political parties that they do not personally support. This is recognised by the **Civil Service Code**, which provides guidelines for civil servants in their work with Ministers, and which has established four main expectations:

*   **integrity** – putting the obligations of public service above personal interests
*   **honesty** – being truthful and open
*   **objectivity** – basing advice and decisions on rigorous analysis of the evidence
*   **impartiality** – acting solely according to the merits of the case and serving governments of different political parties equally well.

(source: http://www.civilservice.gov.uk/about/values/cscode/index.aspx)

If a civil servant pursues a personal agenda against the wishes of the Government of the day, he or she can be dismissed. In fact, most civil servants are professionals whose career advancement would be under threat if they actively went against their political masters.

Special Advisors

Special advisors are staff who are employed to give advice to Ministers but are not members of the Civil Service. Often, they will have previously worked for the Minister when in Opposition or for the Minister's political party. When the Minister or party leaves office, the special advisor will leave too, unlike civil servants, who are permanently employed by the Government no matter which party is in power. Often special advisors will manage the media or public relations approach of the department.

Alastair Campbell

Under recent Governments, concerns have been expressed that the Civil Service has been bypassed in the decision making process. Tony Blair's Director of Communications, Alastair Campbell, was actually appointed to the Civil Service despite not being a professional and having his primary loyalty to Blair and the Labour Party.

Civil servants and special advisors may also give Ministers conflicting advice, due to the fact that they may view policy from different perspectives as well as with different sets of priorities. Tony Blair was accused of relying too heavily on Campbell and his Chief of Staff Jonathan Powell for policy advice, and sidelining Cabinet colleagues and Civil Service experts.

Several controversial episodes have occurred involving special advisors. For example, in April 2009, Gordon Brown's special advisor, Damien McBride, sent an email to a colleague discussing how they could fabricate stories about their Conservative opponents' personal lives. He resigned when the email came to light but an important insight had been gained into the world of special advisors and their activities came under intense scrutiny. Conservative appointees have also courted controversy. Andy Coulson was David Cameron's Director of Communications from 2007 to 2011. Prior to this, however, he was editor of *News of the World*. This coincided with the period in which *News of the World* journalists were involved in hacking the mobile phones of celebrities, including sports personalities and members of the royal family. The paper's royal editor was subsequently found guilty and imprisoned for illegally intercepting private voicemail. While Coulson maintains that he had no knowledge of his journalists' activities, other newspapers suggested otherwise and actually published testimony that implicated him in the scandal. He later resigned his position as Cameron's special advisor because the controversy threatened to damage the Prime Minister himself and, as Coulson claimed, distracted him from his job of serving the PM. These issues partly explain why, for many people, special advisors appear to operate in the shadows: unelected, unaccountable and highly political – an altogether negative influence and the opposite of everything the Civil Servant is supposed to embody.

Top Tip

Try to find out about other controversial episodes involving special advisors.

The Cabinet Office

The Cabinet Office dates back to 1916 when it was founded as a branch of the 'Committee for Imperial Defence' during the First World War. As with other government departments, Ministers are appointed to the Cabinet Office in order to oversee and implement policy. The current Minister for the Cabinet Office is Francis Maude. The Prime Minister is always classed as a Cabinet Office Minister in his or her capacity as **Minister of the Civil Service**. As with other government departments, the Cabinet Office is headed by a non-political civil servant (the **Cabinet Secretary**). The current Cabinet Secretary is Sir Jeremy Heywood, who is also head of the Home (UK) Civil Service; in other words, the head of the Cabinet Office is also the most senior civil servant in Britain.

The Cabinet Office works with the Prime Minister's Office and prepares minutes, agendas and documents to support the work of the Cabinet and government in general. A particular function is to ensure cooperation and coordination across all government departments as well as giving policy advice and helping to manage cabinet committees. The Cabinet Office, however, might pursue a variety of policy objectives set by the current government which are not being handled by other departments. At the moment, Deputy Prime Minister Nick Clegg is a Cabinet Office Minister and is managing the government's agenda on constitutional reform. The resources of the Cabinet Office were directed towards organising a referendum on the introduction of the Alternative Vote System at the start of 2011. The Cabinet Office also manages aspects of national security. For example, the **Joint Intelligence Committee** (containing representatives from the intelligence and security services as well as government) has been part of the department since 1957.

Quick Test 8

1. Outline the powers of the Prime Minister.
2. What are the limits on the power of the Prime Minister?
3. How far does the Cabinet have an input in policy?
4. Explain the difference between civil servants and special advisors.

Parliament

Parliament

The UK Parliament is made up of two components, the **House of Commons** and the **House of Lords**. In centuries past, Lords and aristocrats would sit in the House of Lords while the 'common' people (those of non-aristocratic birth or the younger children of the nobility) would be elected to the House of Commons. Both sought to use Parliament to keep an eye on the power of the monarch and to advance their own interests. Over the past 300 years, Parliament has acquired dominance over the monarchy and the House of Commons has become the primary chamber for legislation and the source of the Government's power.

Top Tip

Although the House of Commons and the House of Lords are collectively referred to as 'Parliament', only Members of the House of Commons are described as 'Members of Parliament' (MPs). Members of the House of Lords are known simply as 'Lords' or 'Ladies' (or peers).

House of Commons

The job of the House of Commons can be summarised as follows:

... must vote on proposed legislation, called **bills**, most of which are introduced by the responsible Government Minister.

... represents the people of the UK. Each MP is elected to speak for and advance the interests of the people of a geographical constituency (currently 650 though due to be reduced).

... must ensure that the Government is 'called to account' for its actions and MPs can question Ministers and the Prime Minister.

The House of Commons ...

... is the branch of Parliament that has the final say over Government spending. Parliament votes on the Government's budget every year, though in practice a Government with a clear majority will have little opposition to its budget.

... is the main arena of debate for Government and Opposition. National issues are debated and opinions aired on behalf of MPs' constituencies.

... is where the main 'pool of talent' comes from for Governments. Most Cabinet Ministers are MPs before they are appointed to Government roles.

The role of MPs

MPs are integral to the work of Parliament. A major part of their job is voting on Bills. Under the British system, governments normally have little difficulty making laws due to their majority in the House of Commons. Governments also introduce the bulk of Bills in Parliament because they control parliamentary time. It is possible for MPs to introduce **Private Members' Bills** into Parliament, but these have little chance of becoming law without Government support.

MPs who are not part of the Cabinet or Shadow Cabinet are known as **backbenchers**. Backbenchers can be influential as members of committees and governments ultimately depend on their support to stay in power.

In the summer of 2009, the *Daily Telegraph* ran a series of articles exposing how many MPs had abused the parliamentary expenses system for their own personal advantage. Former Labour MP Jim Devine falsely claimed £8385 by submitting receipts for cleaning and printing work. The scandal also forced the **Speaker of the House of Commons** to resign. (The Speaker is the MP who is chosen to preside over debates.) Many MPs have since retired and some, like Devine, faced criminal prosecution for fraud. The expenses system has since been tightened up, but the reputation of Parliament and MPs among the public remains low.

How does a Bill become law?

A Bill must proceed through several stages before it becomes an **Act of Parliament** and is made law.

All Bills, other than financial Bills, then go to the House of Lords where they go through the same stages. The final step is for the Bill to receive **Royal Assent**. According to custom, the monarch must approve every Act of Parliament.

The role of the Opposition

The **Opposition** is the collective name given to the MPs of the second largest party in the House of Commons. The Opposition must challenge and scrutinise the work of the Government and hold them to account. Public funds are provided for this purpose.

The Opposition presents itself as an alternative to the current Government, with senior Opposition MPs acting as 'shadows' to Ministers in charge of different Government departments. The Opposition will present alternative policies to that of the Government and seek to slow down its work.

Several criticisms can be made of the Opposition in Parliament:
- They slow down the work of the Government.
- They may misconstrue the policies of the Government for political advantage.
- An Opposition facing a majority government is largely ineffectual, providing the Government's MPs remain loyal.
- The adversarial nature of the House of Commons stresses difference and confrontation rather than cooperation for the benefit of the country (despite promises of a 'new politics' in the wake of the Conservative/Lib Dem Coalition). This is especially evident at Prime Minister's Questions, when the Opposition leader has an extended period of time to ask the PM questions, usually in an attempt to 'score points' for the TV cameras.

> **Top Tip**
>
> The Labour Party are currently the official Opposition to the Conservative/ Lib Dem Coalition. They have a Shadow Cabinet who sit on the front bench facing the Government front bench. For example, Andy Burnham is the shadow Education Secretary. He 'shadows' the actual Education Secretary, Michael Gove.

In order to present itself as a credible alternative to the Government, the Opposition must also be constructive when possible. This can involve proposing credible alternatives to Government policies or even supporting certain Government policies with which they are in agreement. When the major parties are in agreement, this is referred to as a **'cross-party consensus'**. One example of this was Prime Minister Tony Blair's decision to go to war in Iraq in 2003, which was supported even more enthusiastically by the Conservative Opposition than it was by many members of the Labour Government.

How does Parliament hold the Executive to account?

One of the main jobs of Parliament is to ensure that proper scrutiny takes place of Government.
- **Debates:** The House of Commons debates important issues. A key debate took place on the eve of the Iraq war in 2003 before the Government held the crucial vote on whether or not Britain would go to war. Members of the public can now trigger parliamentary debates by signing online Government petitions. At the end of the day, MPs can debate issues on request (Adjournment Debate).

- **Question time:** MPs have the right to question members of the Government. On Wednesday at 12.00pm, backbench MPs and the Opposition have the opportunity to ask the Prime Minister questions. However, PMQ is often rather theatrical and often used by the Opposition to 'score points' from the Government and get 'soundbites' (short snappy quotes) on to the main evening news.
- **Select Committees:** These are small committees of MPs which each examine a specific aspect of the work of the Government. There are Select Committees dealing with Foreign Affairs, the Treasury, Defence and Health among others. MPs are elected to committees and places are allocated proportionally according to a party's overall number of MPs. These Select Committees may take evidence from experts, call the Minister and civil servants for questioning, and publish recommendations. The Culture, Media and Sport committee has had a high profile in the wake of the phone hacking scandal. Chairs of Select Committees can become powerful MPs in their own right. Labour MP Keith Vaz chairs the Home Affairs Select Committee, and will have the job of monitoring the Government's record on policing, crime and immigration.

Keith Vaz

The House of Lords

The UK Parliament is a **bicameral legislature**. This means that it has **two components**: the **House of Commons** and the **House of Lords**. The existence of an Upper House has been particularly appropriate in Britain, with its tradition of strong majority governments based in the House of Commons.

Bills must go through the House of Lords, but the chamber now only has the power to delay Bills, and cannot defeat them, or propose legislation of its own. This still gives the Government time to reflect on any hasty legislation.

The House of Lords can also suggest potential problems with any Bill and ask the House of Commons to reconsider. Under the **Salisbury Convention**, the House of Lords will not vote against the second or third reading of a Bill if it is in the Government's manifesto.

The pomp and ceremony of the House of Lords.

The House of Lords is composed of the following:

Life Peers

They are appointed for the duration of their lives, usually as a reward for government service, and are nominated by political parties. John Prescott, for example, a former Labour Deputy Prime Minister, was appointed to the House of Lords in the summer of 2010, after he stood down as an MP. He is now Lord Prescott of Hull. In 2010 there were 589 Life peers.

Elected Hereditary Peers

Before 1999, many peers sat in the House of Lords by accident of birth: they simply had to be born the eldest child of a noble family. The Labour Government at the time reformed this ancient practice, and removed most of the hereditary peers. Only a few were allowed to remain, providing they had been elected by the other members of the House of Lords. In 2010 there were 90 such peers.

Archbishops and Bishops of the Church of England

As the Church of England is the Established (official) religion of the Kingdom, the Queen remains the Head of the Church of England and senior churchmen have the right to sit in the House of Lords. In 2010 there were 38 such peers.

As in the House of Commons, most members of the House of Lords are organised along party lines. However, they do not represent constituencies and party control is weak. A number of peers have no party affiliation and are called **crossbenchers**. No party has an overall majority in the House of Lords.

The Whip System

As it is difficult to be elected to the House of Commons without being the candidate of one of the main political parties, it is no surprise that political parties play a major role in the House of Commons, and that the party **Whips** are significant figures in a parliamentary party.

It is the job of Whips to ensure that backbench MPs vote in line with the party leadership and the leadership will employ a variety of methods to ensure backbench loyalty. This will involve negotiating and convincing MPs that their leadership's policy is worthy of support. Whips will also employ a 'carrot and stick' approach with MPs. Loyal backbenchers will be rewarded, possibly with promotion to the Cabinet or Shadow Cabinet, while rebellious MPs will be isolated, briefed against to the media, or, as a last resort, have the whip withdrawn. This means that they are expelled from their party and cannot seek re-election as their party's candidate. It is therefore difficult for young and ambitious MPs to vote against their leadership, although some will do so, as when dozens of Conservative MPs defied David Cameron to vote for a referendum on European Union membership in October 2011.

The Whips employ a system to indicate to MPs the importance of their attendance at votes. A 'three line whip' is a signal that MPs must show up to the House of Commons that day and vote with their party. In the case of a 'two line whip', the MP may be excused if they can arrange for an opposite number to abstain from the vote as well. A 'one line whip' simply requests that the MP attends the vote, which may be a routine matter or foregone conclusion.

Although votes on most major issues are managed by the Whips, some issues, such as those of conscience or morality, are traditionally not. Examples include votes on abortion and gay rights, where MPs usually have a 'free vote'.

Quick Test 9

1. What are the main functions of the House of Commons?
2. Describe the role of the Opposition.
3. In what ways can Parliament act as a check on the Executive?
4. Outline the main ways in which the House of Lords is different from the House of Commons.

Influences on decision making

Pressure groups and their methods

Pressure groups are organisations which are dedicated to a particular cause or goal. Although the law is decided in Parliament, pressure groups provide individuals with a way of making their voices heard when decisions are being made. At the same time, pressure groups do not seek power through the electoral system and are therefore different from political parties. They also campaign on a narrow range of issues or even a single issue. This again distinguishes them from political parties which normally have a set ideology and stated positions on all political, social and economic issues.

The activities of Fathers for Justice are examples of pressure group direct action.

Pressure groups fall into different categories. There are **cause groups** and **interest groups.** Cause groups campaign on issues and attract members and supporters who feel passionate about a particular cause. Interest groups, on the other hand, represent the interests of their members. Pressure groups can be classed as **insider** or **outsider** groups depending on how friendly they are with the current government and how much influence they have with them.

Pressure groups will use a variety of methods, both legal and illegal, to influence decision making, and with varying degrees of effectiveness. For example, pressure groups will often **lobby** Government Ministers to convince them that a particular policy or cause is correct.

GROUP	CAUSE OR INTEREST?	INSIDER OR OUTSIDER?	METHODS	EFFECTIVENESS OF ACTIONS
Educational Institute of Scotland	Concerned with the interests of members (teaching staff) such as pay and conditions but also campaigns for Scottish education	Insider	Lobbying Government; giving evidence to parliamentary committees; negotiating with Government and local councils; large scale demonstrations (e.g. March 2010 rally against education cuts in Scotland)	Agreements are usually reached with Government and employers and advice usually given serious consideration.
Stop the War Coalition	Cause group that is against British military involvement in the 'war on terrorism', e.g. the Afghanistan war	Outsider	Large scale demonstrations such as the protest against the Iraq war in 2003 which brought millions out to demonstrate but ultimately failed to prevent the war	No relationship to speak of with Government and any advice would be so contrary to Government policy that it would be ignored. However, they may succeed in influencing public opinion, which could force a change of Government policy.
Taxpayers Alliance	Avowedly an interest group (the interests of UK taxpayers) but also campaigns for less Government spending and lower taxes	An outsider group but closer to insider status when Conservative Party are in power	Media campaigns such as debates on news programmes; publishing research which can be used by sympathetic MPs	High profile presence in media and views are sought out especially in current economic crisis.
Fathers for Justice	Seeks to defend the interests of fathers who have been denied access to their children	Outsider	Direct action: stunts such as climbing on top of important buildings dressed as super heroes	High profile but illegal and dangerous stunts run risk of alienating the public and not being taken seriously.

Case Study

Hugh Berrington, the late Professor Emeritus at the School of Geography, Politics and Sociology at the University of Newcastle upon Tyne, gives his opinion on whether pressure groups are good for democracy.

Like political parties, pressure groups are often attacked for distorting the democratic process. It is true that pressure group activity confers advantages on wealthy, well-organised and well connected groups, and those able to inflict sanctions on government by withdrawing their cooperation.

Yet, as with parties, their contribution to democratic life is indispensable. Dealing as they often do with narrow and specialised issues they are a vital channel between the governed and the governors.

The task of governing a nation of nearly 60 million people, and ensuring some conformity between popular wishes and government decisions, is enormous in its complexity.

To many, especially those at the '*receiving end*' of government decisions it must often seem as though politicians and civil servants follow their own agenda without reference to the people's wishes.

Looking at that task, though, from a more detached vantage point it seems that, as with a dog dancing, the wonder is not that it sometimes seems to be done badly but that it is done at all.

Accessed at http://news.bbc.co.uk/1/hi/programmes/bbc_parliament/2443603.stm

Top Tip

Pressure groups often employ professional **lobbyists** to try to influence the Government.

Top Tip

If the cause of a pressure group arouses particularly strong feeling among members of the public, it can evolve into a political party which can contest elections and seek power, e.g. the Labour Party arose from the trade union movement.

The media and politics

The mass media play a significant role in the decision making process. A massive amount of political information is available from newspapers, 24 hour news, political discussion shows, radio programmes, blogs, websites and social media. While TV must provide balanced coverage, newspapers and blogs are free to take sides.

Newspapers generally have political standpoints or agendas, and newspaper columnists will interpret the facts according to their political sympathies. Often newspapers announce to great fanfare which parties they are backing at election time. Newspapers also present their views in **leading articles**, such as *The Sun Says* or *Record View*. The wide range of newspapers in the UK means that any government will be challenged by the print media.

Newspapers have begun to take on a role as an unofficial opposition to the Government, investigating and exposing what they see as wrongdoing. The Labour Governments from 1997 to 2010 generally faced weak opposition in Parliament and the principal opposition came from the press. Some of the most hostile coverage the Government faced was over the Iraq war and the failure to find weapons of mass destruction in Iraq; much of it, ironically, from the traditionally pro-Labour *Daily Mirror*. In some ways, newspapers are a far more effective opposition than political parties as they reach an audience of millions and their activities are not subject to the same scrutiny as parliamentary opposition. This, however, can sometimes encourage journalists to behave badly in pursuit of their aims. For example, the *News of the World* hacked the phones of many celebrities and politicians. At the same time, it is doubtful that the MPs' expenses scandal would have come to light without the activities of the media.

NEWSPAPER	PARTY SUPPORTED AT 2010 GENERAL ELECTION
Guardian	Liberal Democrat
Sun	Conservative
Daily Record	Labour
Daily Mirror	Labour
Daily Mail	Conservative
Daily Telegraph	Conservative
The Times	Conservative

TV and radio provide an opportunity for journalists to question leading political figures. Key slots include *Question Time* and the '8.10 interview' on the *Today* radio programme; for these slots political parties will normally put forward good media performers to argue their case. Favourable media coverage is a must for a government and has become an obsession for some. Tony Blair employed many special advisors partly in a bid to manage the media which had given Labour poor coverage in the 1980s.

The internet and other **new media** are becoming increasingly influential in politics, particularly at election time. Many politicians have *Twitter* accounts and parties attempt to solicit donations and recruit members through websites. Footage of speeches and meetings can be caught with a mobile phone and placed on *YouTube* within minutes. This means that politicians have to be increasingly careful in what they say and when they say it. During the 2010 General Election, Labour candidate Stuart MacLennan was forced to resign after he made posts on *Twitter* in which he described the elderly as 'coffin dodgers' and made obscene comments about Conservative leader David Cameron and Liberal Democrat leader Nick Clegg.

Top Tip

Government information has become readily available in recent years. Freedom of Information laws have limited what the Government can keep secret, while Wikileaks has shown how new media can expose classified information.

Although TV is officially required to be neutral, some people believe there to be pro-Labour (or left-wing) bias at the BBC and pro-Conservative bias at Sky. One of the most interesting exchanges of the 2010 election was when former Labour spin doctor Alastair Campbell accused the Sky News political editor Adam Boulton of pro-Conservative sympathies, provoking an angry reaction from Boulton.

Live televised debates between the main party leaders have long been commonplace in other democracies. They took place for the first time in Britain during the 2010 election campaign. Previous attempts to organise these had always collapsed, usually because of the intransigence of whichever party leader had the most to lose from a bad performance. Tony Blair initially called for debates then backed away from this position when he amassed a huge lead in the polls. Gordon Brown, trailing in the polls, had little to lose and found a willing opponent in David Cameron. But it was Nick Clegg who captured the public imagination with polished performances in all three debates. Despite making Clegg a household name, the increased support the Liberal Democrats gained from the debates turned out to have evaporated by election night, if it ever existed at all. It is perhaps too early to tell what effect televised debates will have on the outcome of British elections, but at the moment it should not be overstated.

Top Tip

Try to spot media bias the next time you watch or read about a political stories. Who would benefit and what do you think its impact will be?

Quick Test 10

1. What are pressure groups?
2. Describe the differences between cause groups and interest groups.
3. Evaluate the different methods of pressure groups.
4. To what extent are pressure groups good for democracy?
5. What role does the media play during election campaigns?

Electoral systems, voting and political attitudes

To prepare for the exam you should know about the following:

- The advantages and disadvantages of:
  - First Past The Post
  - The Additional Member System
  - The Single Transferable Vote.
- The impact each of these electoral systems has had on UK politics.
- The different factors that influence voting behaviour:
  - Social class
  - Age
  - Gender
  - Ethnicity
  - Issues
  - Party leaders and personalities
  - Geography.

First Past The Post

Voters in the UK are exposed to a number of different electoral systems. The First Past The Post (FPTP) system is used to elect MPs to the Westminster Parliament in London.

The UK is divided into 650 areas called constituencies. (Of these 650 constituencies, **59 are in Scotland**.) **Each constituency elects one person to act as its representative**. To do this, each voter casts his or her vote by placing an X next to the name of the person they would like as his or her MP. **The party with the most MPs usually forms a government**.

Constituencies vary in geographical size. The constituency of Ross, Skye and Lochaber is approximately 12000 square kilometres and is the largest constituency in the UK. The smallest, Islington North in north London, is a mere 735 hectares. The average number of voters in a constituency in the UK is 68175. The largest constituency in terms of voters is the Isle of Wight with over 109000 voters. The smallest is Na h-Eileanan an Iar (the Western Isles) which has only 22000 voters.

In 2010, the largest majority in any constituency was secured by Stephen Timms MP. He held the seat of East Hamwith with a majority of 27826 votes. The smallest majority is in the seat of Fermanagh and South Tyrone – 4 votes.

Advantages of FPTP

- The system is **easy to understand** for voters.
- There is a **clear link between constituents and their MP**.
- **Extremist parties find it difficult** to have MPs elected.
- It *usually* **delivers a majority** for one party and *usually* avoids coalition governments – governments which no-one votes for. The election result in 2010 was the first time, since February 1974, where an overall majority was not held by one party following the election. To have an overall majority, a party in 2010 would have needed to secure 326 seats.

Disadvantages of FPTP

- Many votes are wasted – there are no prizes for coming second. This can discourage some voters from going to the polls.
- Unfair representation.
- Governments are often elected by a minority of voters.
- Lack of choice for voters.
- It leads to negative and/or tactical voting. Voters will often vote for candidates they dislike the least.
- Smaller parties are disadvantaged (see the table below).

UK ELECTION RESULTS 2010			
Party	Seats	% Seats	% Votes
Labour	258	39·7	29
Conservative	307	47·2	36·1
Liberal Democrats	57	8·8	23
Others	28	4·3	11·9

Voter turnout in 2010 was 65·1%. In 2005 it was 61·4%, in 2001 it was 59·4% and in 1997 it was 71·4%. The low turnout in 2001 was largely down to the fact that voters expected Labour to win.

At the 2010 election, there were problems at polling stations in London, Surrey, Manchester, Birmingham, Liverpool, Leeds, Newcastle and Sheffield. Hundreds of voters were unable to vote due to long queues and a lack of council staff. Voters were aware of how close the election polls were running.

To see footage of the voting problems, use an internet search engine to find the footage on the BBC website.

After much deliberation and many talks, the Liberal Democrats agreed to enter into a Coalition Government with the Conservatives. Conservative David Cameron (pictured below on the left) is the Prime Minister, while Liberal Democrat Nick Clegg (below right) is Deputy Prime Minister.

Top Tip

FPTP favours the two large parties. At the 2005 election, Labour polled 35·2% of all votes yet ended up with 55·1% of the seats in the House of Commons.

The two leaders had clashed during the televised debates over certain issues. Two of the main issues they were at odds about were the replacement of Britain's nuclear deterrent – nuclear submarines – and also the issue of immigration.

The Coalition Government was formed after long talks. Nick Clegg was reluctant to form a coalition with Labour – the Conservatives had secured the most votes and seats. Clegg demanded that there be a referendum on voting reform – the Liberal Democrats want FPTP replaced with a more proportional system for electing MPs. A referendum was held in May 2011. Voter turnout was low at just over 40%. 68% of people voted against introducing AV.

Quick Test 11

1. Does FPTP encourage or discourage people from voting at general elections?
2. Which parties do best from the FPTP system?
3. What was unusual about the result of the 2010 election?

Political issues in the United Kingdom

Proportional representation

All proportional representation (PR) systems have positive and negative points. What they all have in common, though, is that the **number of votes** a party receives is more **accurately reflected in the number of seats** it ends up with.

Examples of PR in use around the UK:
* To elect Members of the European Parliament (MEPs): the **Party List System**
* To elect MSPs: the **Additional Member System**
* To elect local councillors in Scotland: the **Single Transferable Vote**
* To elect Members of the Legislative Assembly in Northern Ireland: the **Single Transferable Vote**

The Party List System analysed

The Party List System is an example of proportional representation. Every vote carries the same 'weight' and influence. If a party polls a certain **percentage of overall votes**, the **percentage of seats** they secure will be a very **accurate** reflection of this percentage. On the other hand, the **voter has no say on which person is going to represent them**. The **political parties draw up their own lists** of candidates in order of preference. The **direct link between a constituent and elected representative** – as seen under FPTP – is therefore lost.

The Party List System is **fairer to smaller parties**. Smaller parties, such as the Green Party, are more likely to secure seats under this system. However, the use of the Party List System is more **likely to result in coalitions** coming together in order to form governments. No voter wishes to have their views compromised so this can lead to situations where it is difficult or impossible to get policies passed into law.

Another key issue in regard to the Party List System is that the elected representatives may see themselves as being **accountable to their respective political parties – not the voters who elected them**.

The Party List system – used to elect MEPs – gives voters no say on the individuals who become their representatives. Voters give their support to parties – it is the parties who decide who the representatives are.

Each party draws up a list of candidates, ranked in preference by the political party. Candidates at the top of their party's list have a better chance of being elected.

There can be a national list where the entire country is one constituency, or regional lists where the country is divided up into large multi-member regions. 72 UK MEPs were elected in the European Parliament elections on 4 June 2009. The UK is divided into 12 electoral regions. Each region has between three and ten MEPs and each MEP in a region represents each person living there. At present, Scotland is represented by six MEPs.

Further information on the UK's MEPs can be found on the website: www.europarl.org.uk

In the elections to the European Parliament, a method called the d'Hondt formula is used to allocate seats. Seats are allocated in successive rounds. In each round, votes cast for each party are divided by the number of seats the party has already been allocated in the region plus 1. The party with the highest remaining total in the round wins the seat.

Below is a selection of parties and their performances from the 2009 European elections.

PARTY	VOTES %	MEPS TOTAL	% OF SEATS
Conservatives	27·7	25	35%
United Kingdom Independence Party (UKIP)	16·5	13	18%
Labour	15·7	13	18%
Liberal Democrats	13·7	11	15%
Green Party	8·6	2	3%
British National Party	6·2	2	3%
Scottish National Party	2·1	2	3%
Plaid Cymru	0·8	1	1%
Others	8·5	3	4%

In total, 43·5 million people were eligible to vote at the 2009 European election. Only 15·6 million voted – about a third of voters. The turnout for European elections tends to be low. Many people feel removed from the parliament and are apathetic towards it.

Quick Test 12

1. Explain the way in which MEPs are elected.

2. Compare the % of votes to the % of seats between the UK General Election results of 2010 and the European Parliament results of 2009. To what extent are the European results more proportional?

3. What evidence is there that implementation of PR increases voter turnout?

The Additional Member System (AMS)

PROPORTIONAL REPRESENTATION: ADDITIONAL MEMBER SYSTEM	
Strengths	**Weaknesses**
MSP/Constituent link There is a directly accountable MSP for each constituency.	**MSP conflict** It creates two types of MSP, one with a constituency role and duties, and one without such a base. MSPs are often from different parties.
Proportionality The results are broadly proportional.	**Lack of accountability** Regional List MSPs are not directly accountable to any voters, just to their party leadership, and have no direct constituency.
Strong Government In Scotland the Labour/Liberal Democrat coalition Government introduced policies that demonstrated independence from Westminster (such as free personal care for the elderly).	**Unrepresentative Government** A coalition is likely to result, such as the Labour/Liberal Democrat coalition in Scotland (1999–2007). In return for their support, smaller parties such as the Liberal Democrats may expect several of their policies to be enacted – policies which most voters rejected.
No wasted votes Each voter has at least one effective vote. Even if they see no chance of their candidate winning in the single member constituency, people can use their second vote for a party they support and still have a limited say through an additional member. Conversely, because the first vote does not determine a party's total representation, a voter can use it to express personal support for a candidate without necessarily using the second vote to help that candidate's party.	**Low turnout** It is argued that voters may be confused by new voting systems and so be discouraged from voting. This might be supported by the fact that at Scottish Parliament election turnouts have been: • 1999 58·2 • 2003 49·4 • 2007 51·7 • 2011 50·4 These are consistently lower than FPTP turnouts.
	Power with the parties As in the Party List system, the parties have complete control over choosing their Additional Members.

From *Higher Modern Studies Course Notes* by Irene Morrison, Alan Barclay, George Clarke and Alison Drew (Leckie and Leckie, 2007)

The Additional Member System is a hybrid of two voting systems. It is used to elect MSPs. Each voter has two votes at elections: one vote for a constituency MSP by FPTP and another vote for a party in a regional contest. The parties draw up lists, from which the 'List' MSPs are selected.

73 MSPs are elected to represent constituencies and 56 'List' MSPs represent regions of Scotland. (This is 7 MSPs per region.)

Criticisms of AMS include there being two tiers of MSPs. List MSPs, it could be argued, are more loyal to their respective parties than to the voters who elected them. While not illegal, criticism has also been aimed at the SNP for wording the list vote as being a vote for 'Alex Salmond for First Minister' both in 2007 and 2011.

Why AMS?

The White Paper (proposals), drawn up before the creation of the Scottish Parliament stipulated the use of PR to elect MSPs instead of FPTP. It may seem strange that the Labour Government decided to go against FPTP for the Scottish Parliament – especially as their support in Scotland was strong. If FPTP had been used in 1999, Labour would have ended up with 93 out of 129 MSPs!

The devolved settlement was created to strengthen the UK. Some commentators believed the implementation of AMS would prevent the SNP from gaining an outright majority. The 2011 election has ended this belief. The SNP were successful in winning an outright majority in 2011 by campaigning for 'both votes SNP'.

Top Tip

The d'Hondt method is used to determine the number of List MSPs each party secures. It is a less proportional method than the other popular divisor method, Sainte-Laguë. The d'Hondt method slightly favours large parties over scattered small parties – this contributed to the SNP winning an outright majority in 2011.

The Single Transferable Vote (STV)

STV is used to elect councillors in Scotland. It is also used in Northern Ireland to elect Members of the Legislative Assembly (MLAs).

In Scotland, each of the 32 local authority areas is divided into multi-member constituencies known as **wards**.

Case Study: Highland Council

The Highland Council area has 22 wards. In total, 80 councillors are elected. Of the 22 wards, 14 are represented by four councillors each while 8 wards are represented by three councillors each.

If you live in Inverness Central, you have four councillors who represent you. The number of councillors you have is dependent on the population of the ward in which you live.

Councillors are **elected by voters who place them in order of preference** on their ballot paper. Therefore, a voter would mark the number 1 next to their highest preferred candidate. The voter can then sequentially vote for the other candidates by numbering them (2, 3, 4, etc.). Voters can choose as many or as few candidates as they wish.

The number 1 choice is the most important. If a candidate already has enough votes to secure election, (or too few to stand a chance) the vote will be used to help the next choice of the voter.

STV – strengths and weaknesses

The implementation of STV in Scottish local elections came about due to the 2003 coalition agreement between Scottish Labour and the Liberal Democrats. It saw an end to the use of First Past the Post at Scottish local authority level.

Because wards are represented by between three and four councillors, the likelihood of very small parties securing representatives is slim. However, the creation of three and four member wards did increase the Liberal Democrats' influence on decision making at local authority level. At the same time, it destroyed a great deal of Labour's power, ending the dominance enjoyed by the Scottish Labour Party for many years – particularly in the central belt.

One concern levied at the implementation of STV is that it **broke the constituent/councillor link.** Also, it is a **complex system in comparison to other voting systems**. However, it does give the voter a great deal of **choice** and the notion of a vote being wasted is now far less common.

Quick Test 13

1. Describe the AMS system used to elect MSPs.
2. Explain why AMS was decided upon to elect MSPs.

Why STV for local councils?

The coalition between the Liberal Democrats and Labour in the Scottish Parliament in 2003 only went ahead after Labour agreed to an end to the use of FPTP to elect councillors in Scotland. In doing so, Labour essentially gave up control of many of Scotland's 32 councils – many councils in Scotland are now run by coalitions of different parties.

With councillors in Scotland now being elected using STV, **there is arguably no longer a direct link between a councillor and constituent**. Voters in Scotland, according to which ward they live in, now have three or four councillors. This can be good as there is more chance of there being an elected councillor a constituent voted for.

STV and the UK General Election

If STV had been used to elect MPs at the 2010 UK General Election, the result would have left the House of Commons consisting of:

PARTY	SEATS
Labour	207
Conservative	246
Liberal Democrats	162
Others	35

Top Tip

The use of STV in council elections has reduced the influence of the Labour Party in local government. For example, in 2007 they gained control of only two councils, Glasgow and North Lanarkshire. When FPTP was used in 2003 Labour controlled 13 councils out of 32.

In comparison to the actual result (as shown on page 37), this result would have been far more proportional.

The Alternative Vote (AV)

The Alternative Vote (AV) voting system differs greatly from other forms of PR. It is incredibly similar to FPTP. If AV was used to elect representatives, each constituency would return one elected member. The major difference between FPTP and AV is a voter ranks candidates by number, with a '1' next to their first preference candidate, '2' next to their second preference candidate and so on. They can rank as many or as few at they wish.

Under AV, if a candidate receives a majority of first preference votes then the candidate would be elected. However, if none of the candidates gains a majority of the first preferences, then the second-preference votes of the candidate who finished last on the first count are redistributed. This process is repeated until someone gets over 50 per cent. The Labour Party and Liberal Democrats use AV to vote for their respective party leaders.

PROPORTIONAL REPRESENTATION: ALTERNATIVE VOTE	
Strengths	Weaknesses
Accountability Direct links between voters and single elected representatives are retained.	**Not as proportional as other PR systems** While this system is usually more proportional than FPTP, it would not provide as proportionate results as systems such as the Party List system or AMS.
Tactical voting less likely Each voters can give first preference to the candidate he or she really wants.	**Larger parties are still favoured** Voters who support smaller parties would have little chance of their preferred candidates being elected.
More positive campaigning by parties A party contesting a seat would not want to alienate the supporters of another party's candidate because it may depend on their support to secure over 50%.	**More complex than FPTP** Voters find FPTP easy to understand. Voters may find AV more challenging.

Had AV been used at the 2010 UK General Election, the House of Commons would consist of:

PARTY	SEATS
Labour	262
Conservative	281
Liberal Democrats	79
Others	28

Comparing these figures with the actual result on page 37, the biggest losers would have been the Conservatives and the biggest winners would be the Liberal Democrats. No party would be in a position to form a majority government. AV is more proportionate than FPTP but it is not the most proportional form of PR.

Top Tip

Ed Miliband was elected as Leader of the Labour Party through the use of AV. Only members of the Labour Party, Labour members of the House of Commons, Labour members of the European Parliament and individual members of affiliated organisations, such as trade unions and socialist societies, could vote.

Referenda

A referendum is a direct vote in which everyone who is eligible is asked to either accept or reject a particular proposal or law. On 5 May 2011, a UK-wide referendum was held to find out if FPTP should be replaced with AV. Only 42·2% of those eligible to vote did so. The electorate voted overwhelmingly against the adoption of AV. Had the electorate voted in favour of adopting AV, this decision would have been legally binding and AV would have been used in every General Election from then on.

The question voters were asked was 'At present, the UK uses the "First Past The Post" system to elect MPs to the House of Commons. Should the "Alternative Vote" system be used instead?'

ELECTION RESULTS		
Yes or no	Votes	Percentage
Yes	6 152 607	32·1%
No	**13 013 123**	**67·9%**

Quick Test 14

1. Give one advantage and one disadvantage of STV.
2. Give examples of where AV is used in elections.
3. What is a referendum?
4. Are referenda used frequently in the UK?
5. When was the last Scotland-only referendum held?

Influences on voting behaviour

Social class

Social class is believed to have an influence on voting behaviour. In 1967 political commentator Peter Pulzer said: 'Class is the basis of British politics: all else is embellishment and detail.'

At the time, family structures were far stronger than they are today, with families often sitting down for meals and discussing issues – and politics. It was often said that the 'family which eats together, votes together'. Children would be heavily influenced by parents and would often vote in the same way. British society is broken down in to different 'classes' with people usually identified by their occupations.

> **Top Tip**
>
> Social class can influence voting behaviour. However, there are many other factors which also must be considered and analysed.

The Register-General's Model of Social Class

This model breaks down the population according to occupation. Many statistics are still presented using this model. It breaks down the UK population in the following way:

A Professional occupations

B Intermediate occupations

C1 Non-manual skilled occupations

C2 Manual skilled occupations

D Partly skilled occupations

E Unskilled occupations

In the 1950s and 1960s, class lines were less blurred than they are today. During the 1970s, the two-party (Labour and Conservative) system began to wane. In Scotland, the SNP started to make some inroads. Voter support for the Liberal Democrats increased.

Class dealignment

Traditional class categories began to unravel and blur through the 1980s and 1990s. A former Prime Minister went as far as to say that: **'There is no such thing as society. There are individual men and women, and there are families.'** (Prime Minister Margaret Thatcher, talking to *Women's Own* magazine, 31 October 1987.) Sales of council houses to their occupiers, along with disappearing traditional industries and a growth in the middle class, left Labour losing its traditional support, the working class. In order to win back support (and power), Labour had to change its policies and move away from the ideas of high levels of tax and spend.

Falling political party membership, coupled with reduced income, saw political parties having to identify key groups of voters in order to win elections. Before the 1997 election, allegedly Tony Blair spotted a man polishing his Ford Mondeo and decided he was the kind of 30-something middle income homeowner whom Labour needed to win over from the Tories. 'Mondeo Man' was a man who had perhaps purchased the council house he and his family lived in and, crucially, viewed himself as being middle class. Tony Blair and 'New Labour' were incredibly successful in attracting voters who traditionally voted Conservative. John Prescott, former Deputy Prime Minister, controversially said before the 1997 election that 'we're all middle class now'.

Prior to securing the leadership of his party, Labour Leader Ed Miliband pointed out that 'five million votes were lost by Labour between 1997 and 2010, but four out of the five million didn't go to the Conservatives.

One-third went to the Liberal Democrats, and most of the rest simply stopped voting. It wasn't, in the main, the most affluent, professional voters that deserted Labour either… this represents a crisis of working-class representation for Labour – and our electability.'

While Labour gained support from the A, B and C1 voters – the professional and skilled workers – it also lost support among its traditional working class support. The Conservatives made gains.

		1997 VOTE SHARE	2010 VOTE SHARE	CHANGE
AB	Lab	31%	26%	−5%
	Con	41%	39%	−2%
	Lib Dem	22%	29%	7%
C1	Lab	37%	28%	−9%
	Con	37%	39%	2%
	Lib Dem	18%	24%	6%
C2	Lab	50%	29%	−21%
	Con	27%	37%	10%
	Lib Dem	16%	22%	6%
DE	Lab	59%	40%	−19%
	Con	21%	31%	10%
	Lib Dem	13%	17%	4%

Quick Test 15

1. What is class dealignment?
2. Why did Labour lose support among the working class?
3. What concerns does Ed Miliband have in regard to Labour's support?

Geographic location

Top Tip

Don't generalise in the exam and refer to a north/south divide. The situation is more complex today and you must acknowledge this.

In the past, there was a north/south divide in Britain. The south of England tended to vote Conservative, while the rest of the UK – the north of England, Wales and Scotland tended to elect Labour MPs. Northern Irish politics has a different dimension due to the political situation there.

After the 2010 election, the 650 constituencies of the UK resulted in the election map below:

There are strong regional variations in voting patterns. The Conservatives fared poorly in Scotland in 2010, securing only one seat and therefore returning only one Scottish MP to the House of Commons. Labour's performance in 2010 was an improvement on the 2005 election. The party won back two seats which it had lost at by-elections. The SNP saw their Westminster representation fall from seven to six MPs. This fall came despite Alex Salmond claiming the party was on course to win 20 seats. The SNP had hoped to find themselves in a position of being 'kingmaker' whereby they could get concessions for Scotland.

The Conservatives fared very well in the south of England (with the exception of parts of London). Of note, they made considerable breakthroughs in Wales. The 2010 election also saw history being made with the leader of the Green Party of England and Wales (Caroline Lucas) elected to represent Brighton Pavilion constituency. The Green Party, which won the seat from Labour, had radical policies in its manifesto including road pricing, taxing the rich far more and decriminalising cannabis. Lucas was the only successful candidate from all of the 335 candidates that the party put forward in 2010. The Green Party of England and Wales would like to see electoral reform.

Geographical differences in voting to some extent show some remaining class loyalty – working class people in London and central Scotland tended to vote Labour.

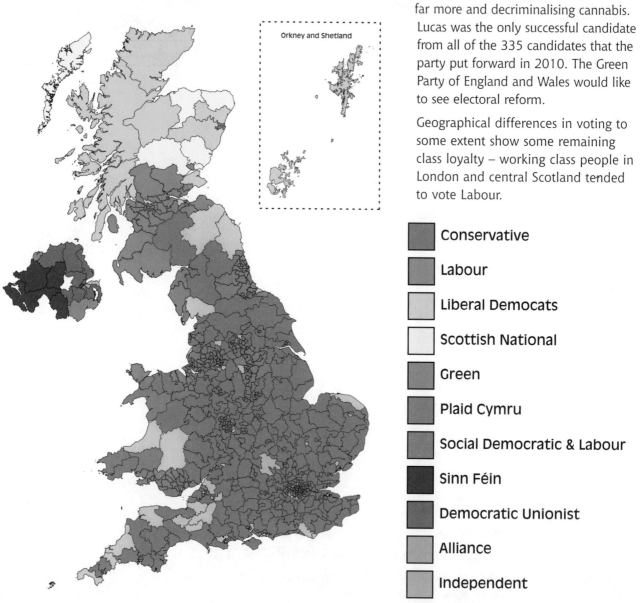

Orkney and Shetland

Conservative

Labour

Liberal Democats

Scottish National

Green

Plaid Cymru

Social Democratic & Labour

Sinn Féin

Democratic Unionist

Alliance

Independent

Gender

Pollsters and election analysts identified a section of society – middle class women – that Labour needed to win over in 1997. 'Worcester Woman' is a political term which describes professional women who worry about issues affecting them and their families directly, education being a key issue. In the past, these middle class voters would have supported the Conservatives, but were persuaded to vote for Tony Blair's Labour Party by the New Labour re-branding. This section of the electorate was particularly targeted during the 1997 and 2001 UK General Election. In 2010, Labour's support among women fell significantly. The election campaigns of all the major parties, but particularly Labour's, were noticeable for the absence of high profile female politicians. This was a marked change from the Labour Party under Tony Blair, who attracted a female vote. Of note, Blair had had an election slogan of 'education, education, education' which appealed to female voters.

In the House of Commons today, only 142 of the 650 MPs are women. This equates to only 22% of MPs being female. There are only four women in the Coalition Cabinet, with one unpaid female member, Baroness Warsi. There are more Liberal Democrat MPs than female MPs in the Cabinet. At the 2010 election, there were 861 female candidates, 21% of all candidates. This figure was up from 2005 (20·3% of candidates were women), and also in 2001 where the figure was 19·3%. Of the main parties, Labour had the highest number and percentage of female candidates.

> **Top Tip**
>
> Women are more likely to vote for female candidates. Barriers to women entering politics include family commitments and a lack of female politician role models. However, party strategists now believe that women hold the key as to who wins and loses elections.

	VOTING IN 2010						CHANGE SINCE 2005				
	Con	Lab	LD	Others	Con lead over Lab	Turn-out	Con	Lab	LD	Turn-out	Con-Lab swing
	%	%	%	%	± %		± %	± %	± %	± %	%
All	37	30	24	9	7	65%	+4	−6	+1	+4	5·0
Gender											
Male	38	28	22	12	10	66%	+4	−6	0	+4	5.0
Female	36	31	26	8	4	64%	+4	−7	+3	+3	5.5

Quick Test 16

1. To what extent did Labour perform well in 2010 in all regions of the UK?
2. Could Caroline Lucas' performance be seen as a success for the Green Party of England and Wales?
3. Did the SNP perform as well as they expected to?

Ethnicity

Of all voters, those from black and other ethnic minority backgrounds **(BME)** are the **least likely to vote.** Voter registration levels among the BME community tend to be below the average rate, with only three out of every four eligible BME voters taking time to register. Experts have identified reasons for this lower level, which include **deprivation** and for many members of the BME community **religious intolerance**. Turnout in constituencies with Conservative MPs is on average 7·3% points higher than in those with Labour MPs. The number of minority ethnic MPs in Parliament is increasing. There are nine more Conservative MPs from a minority ethnic background compared to the previous Parliament and for Labour, the number is up by three. The Conservative Party now has 11 MPs from black and minority ethnic backgrounds, while Labour has 16. The Liberal Democrats are yet to have a minority ethnic MP elected. Overall, the 2010 election saw the total number of MPs from ethnic minority backgrounds almost double, from 14 to 27.

Top Tip

While the BME vote largely goes to Labour, David Cameron has worked hard to woo BME voters, especially in Asian communities.

BME voting behaviour is also influenced by social class, age and issue voting. For instance, **the Iraq War was a hugely significant issue**. In 2005, the Respect Party, which campaigned on the issue of the war, was successful in winning the London seat of Bethnal Green and Bow, unseating Labour's Oona King. The constituency has a high proportion of muslim voters. Respect's

George Galloway

candidate, George Galloway, the leader of the Stop the War Coalition, fought a bitter single issue campaign. Galloway left the Labour Party over his refusal to toe the line over Iraq. At his acceptance speech, he declared: 'Mr Blair, this is for Iraq.' The Respect Party lost the seat at the 2010 election to Labour. At this election, the candidates for the seat of Bethnal Green and Bow won the following numbers of votes:

CANDIDATE	PARTY	VOTES	% OF VOTE	SWING
Rushanara Ali	Labour	21 784	42·9	+8·4
Ajmal Masroor	Liberal Democrat	10 210	20·1	+7·8
Abjol Miah	Respect-Unity Coalition	8,532	16·8	−19.8
Zakir Khan	Conservative	7,071	13·9	+2·0

The AB group of the Asian community is more likely to vote Conservative than Labour. The Liberal Democrats have worked hard to gain support among the younger members of the BME community. In Scotland, the SNP is courting the support of the BME community – especially the Asian community. High-profile members of the SNP, Alex Salmond and Nicola Sturgeon, are often seen at Asian functions and fund-raising dinners.

Issues

Issues have become an important feature of campaigns and election results. In the 2010 election, public funding cuts was a key issue. Other issues which were prominent in the 2010 election included immigration, health and education. Political issues are important to 'floating voters'. Floating voters are people who vote according to candidates' and parties stances on the issues which they feel strongly about. For floating voters, the popularity of party leaders also play a large part in their decision on who to vote for.

Image and personality

TV debates

The 2010 election will be remembered for being the first election where the three main party leaders went head-to-head in three live televised debates. The idea for the debates came from Sky News. These debates were heavily scrutinised by the media. Each of the three debates were hosted by a different media organisation. Each one organised small groups of undecided voters from the key marginal seats. Each of these voters were given a handset on which they registered approval/disapproval or neutral feelings throughout the debate. The output of each handset created a live 'worm' graph throughout the debate, showing a total positive or negative rating. The 'worm' polling was provided by polling company ComRes.

Spin

Political parties employ 'spin doctors' to enable them to put a positive 'spin' on stories which the media cover. (The term comes from the sport of baseball where coaches are employed to help pitchers put spin on the ball and so improve their performance.) Tony Blair's spin doctor and right-hand man was Alastair Campbell. Campbell had previously been the political editor of the *Daily Mirror*. He wrote many of Tony Blair's speeches and 'soundbites'. Soundbites are short and snappy pieces of information which make good headlines. Spin doctors also focus on the image of the party leaders. However, spin doctors' actions can become the headlines at times.

When David Cameron announced his intention to run for the Conservative leadership, the assembled journalists were handed fresh smoothies to reflect the image Cameron wished to promote – the fresh, young candidate.

Top Tip

Due to the electoral system used to elect candidates to the UK Parliament, voters do not vote for a party leader. The Prime Minister is chosen by his or her party. Many people, especially floating voters, vote for a certain party on the basis of that party's leader.

Quick Test 17

1. Describe the issues which middle class women consider to be most important.
2. What issues surround poor voter turnout among the BME community?
3. Why are political parties courting the BME vote?

The media and voting

Party political broadcasts

Most people in the UK get their information on politics from watching television. By law, television must remain **neutral** (although most political parties would claim that television does not do this). Political parties use party political broadcasts to get their message across to voters. While political parties believe that party political broadcasts are important, a survey by Ipsos Mori found that nearly three-quarters (74%) of those polled agreed that paying household bills is preferable to watching party political broadcasts. While many people turn the channel over when a party political broadcast comes on television, fewer than 20% think they should be banned.

Newspapers

Newspapers are often biased, showing support of certain political parties. Evidence shows that voters will read newspapers which support their political views. The newspaper with the largest daily readership in the UK is the *Sun*. The *Sun* officially endorsed the Conservatives on 30 September 2009. From that point on, the *Sun* was dedicated to a Labour defeat and to a Conservative victory.

TWELVE years ago, Britain was crying out for change from a divided, exhausted Government. Today we are there again. In 1997, "New" Labour, shorn of its destructive hard-Left doctrines and with an energetic and charismatic leader, seemed the answer. Tony Blair said things could only get better, and few doubted him. But did they get better? Well, you could point to investment in schools and shorter hospital waiting lists and say yes, some things did – a little. But the real story of the Labour years is one of under-achievement, rank failure and a vast expansion of wasteful government interference in everyone's lives.

www.thesun.co.uk/sol/homepage/news/2661063/The-Sun-Says-Labours-lost-it.html

Tony Blair had worked hard to win over the support of the *Sun*'s owner, Rupert Murdoch. Rupert Murdoch owns the *Sun* and *The Times* newspapers (among many other media interests). The *Sun* had made claims in the past of being a major influence on people voting. It even claimed after the 1992 election that it was 'the Sun wot won it'.

The *Sun*, 30 September 2009

At the 2007 Scottish parliamentary elections, the *Sun* came out against the Scottish National Party, running a front cover on the day of the election showing a hangman's noose. Despite this front cover, the SNP still went on to win the election. John Curtice, Professor of Politics at Strathclyde University, believes that this front cover had a negligible effect on voters. On the Sunday before election day, four newspapers came out backing Alex Salmond – the *Scotsman* followed suit on the following Monday. There is a strong argument which points to newspapers backing the party which has the best chance of winning. This was evident in the 2011 election campaign when the Scottish *Sun* ran with the headline 'Play it again Salm' in support of Alex Salmond.

The internet

Without doubt, Barack Obama's 2008 Presidential campaign made UK political parties take note of the power of the internet. Political parties in the UK even hired some of Obama's advisors. David Cameron made regular vodcasts on YouTube. The Conservative Party created its own channel on YouTube: www.youtube.com/user/webcameronuk. David Cameron used webcameron to try to show voters he was a normal, family man. However, if you look at the channels that the political parties created, you will see that the videos haven't had a huge number of hits. These videos were more successful in influencing other forms of media – TV and print especially – as opposed to voters directly.

Every party has websites, but, during the 2010 election campaign, they used the internet differently, with social networking sites such as *Twitter* and *Facebook* used extensively. Two of the most popular people linked to the election who were followed on *Twitter* were Sarah Brown (Gordon Brown's wife) and John Prescott.

Smaller parties (with lower levels of finance) such as the Scottish Green Party, utilise social networking to get their messages across and interact with voters. Patrick Harvie, Co-convener of the Scottish Green Party, tweets frequently.

> **Top Tip**
>
> If you've got a *Twitter* account, you can follow the party leaders online to find out what they're doing. Your local MP, MSPs and councillors may also have an online presence. Social networking is changing the way elections are fought by parties.

Caroline Lucas, the first Green Party of England and Wales candidate elected to Westminster, used *Facebook* and *Twitter* extensively to secure the seat of Brighton Pavilion at the 2010 UK General Election.

On 8 May 2010, when William Hague announced the restart of Conservative/Liberal Democrat coalition talks, he did so via *Twitter*. Out of all 650 MPs, 198 MPs and five Cabinet Ministers tweet regularly. Some even tweet live from the debating chamber of the House of Commons.

Feeding into the TV debates, many younger voters used social networking sites to discuss the leaders' performances and the policies which they were conveying. The turnout for the 18–24 age group was **up by 7% on the 2005 election** – this group is the most active in terms of social networking sites.

Social media case study

Ewan McIntosh, CEO and founder of consultancy firm 'NoTosh' worked on the 2011 SNP digital campaign. When he started working on this campaign, exactly 100 days prior to polling day, all polls indicated that the Labour party were set to win. At one point during the campaign the SNP were 15 points behind Labour.

McIntosh advised the SNP on how to harness social media to convey their manifesto ideas in tandem with offline media. A key element was breaking their manifesto down in to small mini-manifestos to target certain groups of voters and using television debate discussions on Twitter, and Facebook advertising, to reach out to many small, targeted groups in the last weeks of the campaign.

The SNP digital team also helped senior party figures set up Twitter accounts and showed them how to use Twitter. This helped the SNP connect with voters directly. Party supporters could also re-tweet links.

Further reading on Ewan McIntosh's involvement can be found at http://bit.ly/jlbkFd

At the 2010 election, the Electoral Commission's website – www.aboutmyvote.co.uk – recorded 1·8m visits, 40% of them from 18–24 year olds. This was a record level of engagement for the Electoral Commission.

The ease of up-to-date information is useful to voters. Most major news organisations now have news apps. While news sources are many, and at the moment mostly free, the shift among news outlets is towards charging readers for use of websites.

Quick Test 18

1. To what extent are party political broadcasts effective?
2. What evidence exists to support the view that newspapers back the party which has the best chance of winning?

The causes of poverty

To prepare for the exam you should know about the following:
*   The background to the welfare state.
*   Inequalities in wealth; causes and consequences of inequalities in wealth; and the effectiveness of Government responses to deal with these inequalities.
*   Inequalities in health; causes and consequences of inequalities in health; and the effectiveness of Government responses to these inequalities.
*   The particular impact of poverty and inequality on women and ethnic minorities.
*   The principles of the welfare state; the debate over the provision of and funding of healthcare and welfare. You should also be aware of the debate over individual and collective responsibility.

Top Tip

Remember that the major theme of this topic is **inequality** – differences between the health, wealth and life chances of different individuals and the reasons for these.

Background to the welfare state

William Beveridge, credited with establishing the modern welfare state.

In 1942, during the Second World War, a civil servant named **William Beveridge** published a report on the future of welfare and social services in Britain. It named **five giant evils,** which government should aim to conquer: **Ignorance, Squalor, Idleness, Want and Disease**. The report was popular and captured the public mood. It was felt that, as ordinary people were bearing the brunt of fighting the war, they should have a brighter future to look forward to when it was finally won. There should be a government safety net from 'the cradle to the grave' where citizens had the right to employment, insurance against poverty, decent housing and education, and a system of medical treatment which was free to those who needed it. In the 1945 election, the Labour Party won a resounding victory on a promise of enacting most of Beveridge's recommendations and in the following years they built on the existing network of social services to create a **welfare state**, with the **National Health Service** (NHS) at its pinnacle.

Top Tip

A useful website is that of the Joseph Rowntree Foundation: www.jrf.org.uk. Read some of the articles and reports related to wealth and health inequalities. Use the information, for example, for background knowledge in Paper 2.

Income and wages

An individual's wages will, to a large extent, determine his or her life chances. Growing inequality in wages has resulted from:
*   The decline of traditional well-paying industries such as shipbuilding and car making (de-industrialisation) and their replacement by service sector jobs, which tend to be lower paid (e.g. call-centre jobs).
*   A growth in part-time and temporary jobs, which tend to be low paid and insecure.
*   The decline in the negotiating power of trade unions, which has made it difficult to secure higher wages.

Many traditional Scottish industries no longer exist.

Top Tip

The median gross annual salary in Britain today is just over £25 000. Anyone who lives on 60% or less of this is classified as living in **relative poverty**, which means being poor in relation to the rest of society.

Today, nearly 4 million people are in low-paid work, and therefore struggle to meet their needs.

Examples of Government action on this problem

- The Labour Government introduced the **National Minimum Wage (NMW)**, currently £6.08 if over 21. However, many trade unions still believe the NMW is too low and campaign for a higher **Living Wage**. The Scottish Labour manifesto in 2011 promised this for public sector workers.
- The Government pays a variety of benefits including **tax credits**, **housing benefit** and **state pensions** to support those on low incomes and other vulnerable groups.

While the percentage of **Gross Domestic Product** (a measure of a country's wealth) spent on these programmes has increased over the past ten years, state benefits have fallen relative to average wages. Pensions and other benefits are **index-linked**. (This means they rise in line with inflation.) They are not linked to wages, which leads to greater inequality between those in work and those dependent on state benefits. The Coalition Government has decided to restore the link between pensions and wages, but its decision to freeze **child benefit** will result in a reduction in income for families with children.

The tax system

There is inequality in the tax system.

- As proportions of their income, the rich pay less than the poor. The current top rate of income tax is 50% for individuals earning £150000 a year or more. In the 1970s, the top rate was 83%. Since 1979, both Conservative and Labour Governments have cut **direct taxation** and increased **indirect taxation**.
- Examples of indirect taxation include **Value Added Tax (VAT)** and duty on alcohol, cigarettes and petrol. This tends to penalise working people who spend a far greater proportion of their income on these items. The current Conservative-Liberal Democrat government increased VAT from 17·5% to 20% in January 2011. It is estimated that the 2011 VAT increase will cost the poorest 10% of people in the UK around 2% of their income compared to a cost of less than 1% for the richest 10% of the population.
- **Inheritance Tax** is paid by owners of estates upon their death. Supporters of the tax argue that wealth inequality is perpetuated if significant sums of money or assets are passed on to the family members of the wealthy. However, some people argue that Inheritance Tax should be abolished as many avoid paying and it is no longer a tax on the super-wealthy. In 2004 approximately 30000 estates paid it, but by 2007 it had increased to 37000, with some of the increase made up of average earners who had saved all their lives.

Top Tip

The **Gini Coefficient** is a measure of income inequality; the nearer to 0 the more income is evenly distributed. In 1979 the UK had a rating of 26 but by 2010 it was 34. In other EU countries it is lower: (e.g. Germany 27, Sweden 33).

Examples of Government action on this problem

- The Coalition Government is raising the level at which people begin to pay tax and they aspire to raise the threshold to £10000 by 2015. This would mean that no one would pay any tax on the first £10000 of earnings. At the same time, however, **National Insurance contributions** have risen. Chancellor George Osborne has been accused of giving with one hand and taking away with the other.
- The Coalition Government is continuing with Labour's policy of tax credits. There are two types of tax credits: working tax credits and child tax credits. If a household has an income below £41000 it is entitled to child tax credits. The working tax credit will be reformed and become the **Universal Credit** in 2016.
- In 2011, Iain Duncan Smith, Secretary of State for Work and Pensions, announced major welfare reform with the Universal Credit. It will replace various means-tested benefits, for example, jobseeker's allowance, housing benefit and working tax credit, with one single universal payment. It is hoped that the Universal Credit will reduce the benefits bill and help people into work and out of poverty.

Unemployment

Unemployment is a major cause of poverty. Currently 2·43 million British people (7·7% of the population) are unemployed. While 1·49 million people claimed Jobseeker's Allowance in May 2011, the highest figure since 1996, there were only 0·5 million job vacancies.

The level of unemployment is influenced by a number of factors, including:

- **The economic cycle**: The current recession means banks have been lending less money so companies find it difficult to expand or create new jobs. Many people cannot get mortgages, resulting in less demand for new houses and therefore unemployment in the construction industry.
- **Government cuts in spending**: An estimated 500 000 jobs are to be cut in the **public sector** (government jobs) because the Coalition Government has reduced public spending.
- **Reliance on service sector jobs, for example call centres and tourism**: These jobs are usually insecure.
- **De-industrialisation**: This refers to the collapse of traditional heavy industries, such as coal mining and shipbuilding. Older people who have skills in traditional trades are unlikely to get jobs in new industries.

Examples of Government action on this problem

There are a range of benefits available through the welfare state to ensure people are supported when out of work.

- The **Employment and Support Allowance (ESA)** is paid to people who have illnesses or disabilities which severely affect their ability to work. The aim of ESA is to help people return to work with a range of support and help. Claimants will have access to specially trained advisers who will offer a range of services including **work-focused interviews**. A new medical assessment has been introduced, the **Work Capability Assessment**. This assesses what people can do, rather than what they cannot, and then identifies the sorts of health-related support they need to return to work. Approximately 7% of adults cannot work due to ill health, and receive benefits such as ESA.
- The current Government is attempting to improve conditions for business so more jobs are created in the private sector. However, they will also cut hundreds of thousands of jobs in the public sector.
- The **Jobseeker's Allowance (JSA)** is the latest name for unemployment benefit. It is designed to encourage people to find work by only providing enough money for a minimum living standard. Currently, the maximum JSA payment for a single person aged 25 or over is £67·50 per week. While this is not sufficient to provide a high standard of living, other benefits are available to supplement unemployed people's incomes.
- The **New Deal** is a project introduced by the Labour Government that originally targeted youth unemployment (18 to 24 year olds). Each claimant was assigned an advisor to support them in finding work. The Labour Government expanded this to other groups:
  - New Deal 25+
  - New Deal 50+
  - New Deal for Disabled
  - New Deal for Musicians (for aspiring unemployed musicians).

If a person refused to participate in the New Deal, his or her benefits could be withdrawn. Critics claimed that its impact on unemployment was minimal; for example, one-third of participants left the New Deal without a job.

The New Deal was changed in 2009 to the Flexible New Deal. The Flexible New Deal is delivered for Jobcentre Plus by 'Providers': professional organisations which offer support tailored to meet individuals' needs. It includes creating action plans to improve people's chances of finding employment and four weeks work experience. Flexible New Deal can last for a year.

Top Tip

Employment Support Allowance is a controversial topic that is typical of the type of issue you may be asked to tackle in a DME. (See page 64.)

Family breakdown as a cause of poverty

Lone parents are more vulnerable to poverty than other types of family:
- Nearly 90% of lone parents are female, making this a gender inequality issue. Furthermore, two thirds of the 4 million people on low pay are women who are working part-time in low-skilled jobs. Some of these women will be lone parents, making them and their children vulnerable to poverty.
- It is widely accepted that children benefit from the stability of having two parents. For example, children from lone parent families are more susceptible to low achievement levels at school.
- Lone parent families have only one breadwinner as opposed to two.

Examples of Government action on this problem

- The UK Government introduced **Working Tax Credits** to make work more financially viable. These are tax refunds paid to working families and are of particular benefit to single parents, who may claim a childcare tax credit worth up to 70% of childcare costs.
- Conservative policy at the 2010 General Election was to introduce a cash bonus for married couples. This policy of 'recognising marriage through the tax system' was ditched in the Coalition agreement.

Gender and race inequality

Women and ethnic minorities may suffer from problems, which can limit opportunities for employment and promotion:
- **High cost of childcare** for single parents and working mothers.
- **Pregnancy and career breaks** can lead to missed promotion opportunities. Women with university degrees face a 4% loss in lifetime earnings as a result of motherhood, while mothers with no qualifications face a 58% loss.
- Britain had the lowest proportion of female engineers in the EU. A World Economic Forum Report suggested that Britain is ranked 42nd in the world in terms of female access to professional jobs and overall wage equality. This represented a drop of ten places between 2007 and 2008. It is often said that a **glass ceiling** prevents women from gaining promotion – despite the fact that they have the qualifications and no formal barriers are in place.
- There is a **pay gap between the earnings of men and women**. In 2010, women earned on average 10% less than men in the UK, (The difference is doubled for women aged 40 or more.) This is despite the fact that girls from all ethnic groups outperform boys in education.
- **Racial discrimination** may be a reason for high levels of ethnic minority unemployment: in the UK in 2010, 48% of blacks aged 16–24 were unemployed, compared to 20% of young whites. In 2010 nearly three-quarters of Bangladeshi children, and half of black African children in Britain were growing up in poverty.
- **Family breakdown**. Black families are more likely to be single parent families than any other group, resulting in lower incomes. However, British Chinese and Indian families typically are two-parent households, often with three generations living together. This reduces the risk of poverty.
- **Language barriers and non-integration**. There is increasing concern that Britain is becoming a fragmented society and that the 'multicultural' project has failed. Some immigrants do not speak English well and this limits their employment opportunities.
- **Occupational segregation**. A 2008 report by the Chartered Management Institute and Department of Work and Pensions, and Institute of Employment Studies, found that around a third of Asian managers and 20% of black managers say racial prejudice and discrimination harm their career progression.

Examples of Government action on this problem

- The **Human Rights Act, 1998** means that British courts must interpret legislation in a way that is compatible with the **European Convention on Human Rights (ECHR)**. The act bans discrimination on the grounds of race, gender and religion.
- The **2003 Race Relations Act** introduced a duty for companies and the public sector to set targets for recruiting more ethnic minority workers. For the first time, the police were subject to its provisions.
- The **Nationality, Immigration and Asylum Act, 2006** introduced a **citizenship test** to try to better integrate immigrants into British life. This was partly in response to panic over Islamic extremism and non-integration.
- The Coalition Government has inherited the **Equality Act, 2010** from Labour. This has brought together all previous laws which cover discrimination and has strengthened them in many areas.

Top Tip

Not all ethnic minority groups suffer the same rates of inequality. British Chinese and Indian people have higher rates of employment and managerial positions than British Pakistani, Bangladeshi and African people.

The record of anti-discrimination legislation is mixed. Over the past twenty years there has been a huge increase in **Black and Minority Ethnic (BME)** achievement. The England football team contains several superstars of black or racially mixed origin, although Asians have yet to make their mark on the national sport. The number of BME and female MPs has risen at every election. However, there are still huge problems with gaps in achievement and equality between the races and sexes. **Many women still face the prospect of hitting a 'glass ceiling' with regard to promotion at work**. How much is caused by prejudice is open to debate. The Equality Act has been criticised for promoting **reverse discrimination** of white men while the Government's citizenship tests have been portrayed in the media as something of a joke.

The fact that the England football team was racially mixed was not the reason that they were heavily criticised during the 2010 World Cup.

Coalition welfare reforms

On 16 February 2011, the Welfare Reform Bill was introduced to Parliament by the Conservative/Liberal Democrat Coalition Government. It aims to introduce a wide range of reforms to make the benefits and tax credits system fairer and simpler, by creating the right incentives to get more people into work by ensuring work always pays. A large part of this would be a 'Universal Credit' which would replace all existing benefits. It would bring together different forms of income-related support to provide one single benefit and would consist of a basic personal amount (similar to the current Jobseeker's Allowance) with additional amounts for disability, caring responsibilities, housing costs and children. As an individual's earnings rose, his or her Universal Credit would be reduced.

Some consequences of poverty

Poverty negatively affects individuals and families. Economic inactivity costs the country billions in welfare payments and there are even higher social costs. Some examples of the effects of poverty are:

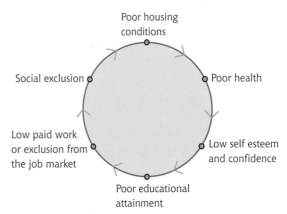

The vicious cycle of poverty

- **Individuals in poverty are likely to suffer from poor mental and physical health**
  Research has established a link between unemployment and deterioration in physical health, depression and suicide. Some people abuse alcohol, drugs and smoke heavily to deal with poverty and depression. This has a negative impact on physical health and life expectancy.

- **Social exclusion**
  This refers to individuals and families being unable to play a full part in society, often due to poverty and low income. Parents, for example, may be unable to pay for school trips for their children, leaving them excluded from other children's activities. The elderly are also vulnerable to social exclusion. Elderly people may live alone and suffer from poor mobility, leaving them with little or no access to friends, family and even public services.

- **Educational underachievement**
  Education may not be a priority in low-income families as parents prioritise paying for necessities such as housing and food. Low-income families may also have problems such as lack of confidence, drug abuse, alcoholism and involvement in crime which undermine children's chances at school. These children may be sucked into a 'cycle of poverty' where their circumstances lead to low attainment in education, which in turn denies them their clearest route out of poverty and social exclusion.

- **Poor quality housing/homelessness**
  Poor housing is related to low income which, in extreme cases, can result in homelessness. When new standards for housing were introduced in England in 2007, a third of houses were classified as **non-decent**. Areas with poor-quality housing are linked to high crime rates, drug abuse and health problems which perpetuate the 'cycle of poverty'. With cuts to Scotland's block grant from Westminster, there has also been a decrease in house-building projects, which has made the problem of lack of affordable housing worse. There is also a shortage of council housing. A great number of council houses were sold during the 1980s and 1990s to the tenants who lived in them. This left a shortage because new council houses were not built to replace those that were sold.

Quick Test 19

1. Describe the main causes of poverty.
2. Why are women and ethnic minorities vulnerable to poverty?
3. How effective have Government policies been in reducing poverty and tackling inequality?
4. Give two examples of the impact that poverty can have on a person's life.

The causes of health inequalities

The NHS today

The National Health Service is an integral part of the welfare state. It was founded on the principles of being free at the point of use and funded by taxation. It is therefore a prime example of a collectivist approach to tackling inequality. The NHS aimed to eliminate the giant of disease (poor health) and it was phenomenally successful – a victim of its own success. Life expectancy in Britain is today 79 for women and 77 for men. However, this has been at great expense: **the NHS cost £110 billion in England in 2010**.

The NHS is today a very different organisation from that which was established in 1948 following the Beveridge Report.

- Charges for certain services such as prescriptions have been introduced to help meet rising costs.
- **There is no longer one NHS**. With the creation of devolved assemblies for Wales and Northern Ireland, and the Scottish Parliament, each region of the UK has focused on different priorities.
- In 2006, free eye tests were re-introduced in Scotland. The SNP Government also abolished all **prescription charges** in 2011. This has come under fire from opposition parties in the Scottish Parliament: they argue that although the policy is popular and vote-winning, it is not a good use of health resources. The SNP counter that it is in keeping with the founding principles of the NHS and the welfare state.

Scottish Health Secretary Nicola Sturgeon has defended her Government's decision to abolish prescription charges.

> **Top Tip**
>
> When asked to evaluate Government policies aimed at reducing health inequalities, do not simply discuss the NHS. You must be prepared to discuss in detail the various local, regional and national health policies that the Government has introduced, both through the NHS and independently of it, and come to a conclusion on each policy's success.

- As of June 2011, the NHS in England is in the process of major reform, with the **NHS and Social Care Bill** planning to devolve much more individual responsibility to GPs and individual patients as 'consumers' of healthcare. This marks a break with Labour's more collectivist policy which involved massive increases in NHS funding and top-down control of health policy.
- The NHS is divided into **primary care** and **secondary care** providers. Dentists and local GPs are examples of primary care providers while the planned and emergency care provided by hospitals and self-governing **Foundation Trusts**, which manage their own budgets and set their own priorities, are examples of secondary care.

Despite over 60 years of the NHS, the UK remains a society that is unequal in health. The **Black Report** (1980) was the first academic study to establish a link between poverty and poor health. Many Government policies and initiatives have attempted to address this problem but they have had mixed success. This is evident in the Marmot Review (2010), which again highlighted the negative impact poverty has on health. There are many reasons for persistent inequalities in health.

Lifestyle choices

- Many people would argue that poor lifestyle choices are the primary causes of poor health. It is argued that people ultimately choose to smoke, eat poorly or drink too much alcohol. According to Cancer Research, around 86% of all lung cancer deaths in the UK are caused by smoking.
- A report by the Association of Public Health Observatories found that the UK had one of the highest obesity rates in the EU and that in Scotland around 25% of adults were obese. Obesity can result in a host of health problems such as cancer, heart disease and diabetes.

Examples of Government action on this problem

- **Smoking ban**
  This was introduced in Scotland on 26 March 2006. It banned smoking in public places where it was still socially acceptable, such as pubs and restaurants. Figures from the Scottish Government show that there has been a 17% fall in heart attacks since the ban was introduced.
- **Action on alcohol abuse**
  The SNP Government attempted to crack down on alcohol misuse by proposing minimum pricing per unit of alcohol and increasing the age that alcohol could be purchased in supermarkets from 18 to 21. Both of these measures were defeated during the SNP's period in minority government as opposition parties successfully argued that they punished responsible drinkers. However, the new SNP government plans to reintroduce these proposals. The Scottish Government has also run anti-alcohol campaigns.
- **Health-promoting schools**
  Schools in Scotland are under a legal obligation to ban fizzy drinks and sweets from their grounds. Vending machines selling unhealthy snacks have been removed and 'Fuel Zones' now sell nutritious food to Glasgow schoolchildren. However, schools can still do little about older pupils visiting ice cream vans and fast food shops at lunchtime. The blanket ban on confectionary (including in tuck shops) has led to criticism of overreaction and 'nannying'.

Geography, social class, and ethnicity

- Statistics show that those in social class AB (for example doctors) have a life expectancy of around seven years more than those in social class DE (for example cleaners).
- Geography is linked to social class as some areas have far higher rates of socioeconomic deprivation (high unemployment, poor housing, low-paid jobs). There is a geographical divide within a number of British cities. **Life expectancy in the Glasgow East End community of Calton is 54 but in Lenzie (to the north-east of the city) it is 82**. This is linked to inequalities in wealth and class differences – unemployment in Calton is around 10% compared to 3% in Lenzie, where poverty and low incomes are also rare. There are also marked differences in health and life chances between the neighbouring Glasgow communities of Bearsden and Drumchapel.

Obvious inequality: the Glasgow areas of Lenzie and Calton are geographically close, but very different socially.

- Geography and social class inequalities are also linked to lifestyle – 52% of people in Calton smoke compared to the Scottish average of 25%. People in more affluent areas tend to seek help for health problems, therefore reducing the possible risks of illness.

- Health-related lifestyle factors vary greatly across ethnic groups. Different ethnic groups exhibit different behaviours which contribute to increased health risks. Evidence from the EHRC report shows that **Pakistani and Bangladeshi groups are more likely to suffer from poorer health than other ethnic groups**, whereas Chinese men and women have the best overall health.
- Death-rates from strokes, cardiovascular diseases and heart disease are particularly high for Pakistani- and Bangladeshi-born men and women. However **white men are more likely to be overweight or obese** than women but, among Pakistani, Bangladeshi and Black African populations, women are more likely to be overweight or obese than men. Therefore, inequalities exist for all ethnic groups.
- Men born in South Asia (e.g. Bangladesh, Pakistan and India) are 50% more likely to have a heart attack or angina than men in the rest of the UK population. By contrast, men born in the Caribbean are 50% more likely to die of a stroke than the rest of the UK population. All BME groups are more likely to suffer from diabetes than white British. Overall, cancer rates tend to be lower in BME groups. Lung cancer mortality rates are lower in people from South Asia, the Caribbean and Africa, which relates to lower levels of smoking.
- The highest mortality rate is found in people from Northern Ireland and Scotland. Mortality from breast cancer is lower for migrant women than for women born in England and Wales. Researchers think this reflects the fact that it takes time to acquire the detrimental lifestyle and other risk factors associated with living in the UK.

Examples of Government action on this problem

- **Healthy Living Centres** were established to help 'hard to reach' groups in deprived communities. These draw together various services and offer a range of activities. The Glasgow East End Healthy Living Centre offers football, zumba and yoga, in addition to a crèche and nursery for local people.
- **Have a Heart Paisley** was established in 2000 to prevent heart disease in the local area. It particularly targets its early intervention at deprived social groups and those aged 45–60.
- **Sure Start Centres** offer health advice and services to mothers with infant children. Assistance offered includes childcare advice, breastfeeding advice and parenting advice, in addition to some health services. Sure Start Centres in deprived communities have additional resources to meet their more complex needs.

Environment

The area in which a person lives can have a big impact on his or her health. If the area is deprived, health problems related to poor quality housing increase. For instance, 10% of the poorest households in Scotland do not have central heating. This increases the risk of health problems such as asthma and bronchitis – both are caused and made worse by dampness.

Examples of Government action on this problem

- Glasgow Housing Association was established in 2003 to manage Glasgow City Council's stock of council houses. Tens of millions of pounds have since been invested in building work and upgrading and housing across the city has been transformed. Places such as Easterhouse have been transformed from areas of slum housing to communities with modern, attractive accommodation.

Age

- The healthiest section of the population is between the ages of 16 to 45. The reality of getting older is that bodies begin to deteriorate. The least healthy group in society is people over 65.
- Research has shown that 50% of the poorest over-75s have long-standing illnesses or disabilities, compared to only one-third of the richest over-75s.
- Illnesses common in old age include arthritis, heart disease, Alzheimer's disease and hypothermia.

Examples of Government action on this problem

- **Free personal care for the elderly** has been a flagship policy of the Scottish Government. Elderly people in Scotland no longer have to pay for care, e.g. in a nursing home.
- The elderly also benefit from **winter fuel payments**, which are one-off cash payments from central government of up to £300 to over-65s to heat their homes in winter. This is to prevent **fuel poverty** and health problems, such as hypothermia and asthma, arising from poor housing. As the payment is **not means tested**, all elderly people qualify, including well-off people, who may have few health or financial problems. It could be argued that this is a waste of money.

Top Tip

Remember that causes of health inequalities are interconnected. Poor lifestyle choices are likely to be made by people who are poorer and who live in disadvantaged areas of cities.

The elderly in Scotland no longer have to sell their homes to meet the cost of their care.

Quick Test 20

1. What is the link between income and health?
2. How can lifestyle choices lead to poor health?
3. Describe some of other causes of health inequalities.
4. Give examples of Government responses to health inequalities.
5. Divide the different government policies under three headings: Local Government, Scottish Government, Central Government.
6. Explain in detail the ways in which the causes of health inequalities are interrelated.

Individualist and collectivist views of the welfare state and NHS

Opinions on the welfare state and the NHS can be broadly divided into two categories: **individualist** and **collectivist**.

Individualist

Individualists believe that government interference in people's lives should be reduced.

David Cameron is more individualist than collectivist.

- The Conservative Prime Minister, **David Cameron**, is far more individualist than his Labour predecessor, **Gordon Brown**.
- The current NHS reforms of the Conservative-led Coalition are decidedly individualist as they encourage more individual activity and responsibility.
- However, the Conservatives have drastically changed their outlook from the days when they denied that a person's circumstances had anything to do with their life chances. In the 1980s they dismissed the findings of the Black Report. Today, they accept that some people are poor or unhealthy through no fault of their own.
- Some individualist thinkers have suggested that people can be **nudged** into making better individual choices, e.g. giving up smoking, working hard, etc, rather than being lectured or told what to do by a **'nanny state'**.

Collectivist

- Collectivists believe that taxation should be high and the better-off should pay for the welfare and healthcare of the less fortunate.
- The policies of New Labour, under both Tony Blair and Gordon Brown, were far more collectivist.
- The collectivist approach involves the government taking responsibility for healthcare and individual welfare, with higher levels of welfare and health spending, and more interference in people's lives with the aim of improving them.
- The smoking ban is an example of a collectivist policy.
- The welfare state and NHS were founded on the collectivist principle of government care 'from the cradle to the grave'.

Case study 1: Individualist and collectivist views of private healthcare

Private healthcare refers to any healthcare that is consumed or purchased outwith the NHS. The individualist view is that it skips NHS waiting times and frees a place on the NHS for a person who cannot meet the cost of quick treatment. Individualists have no problem with this as they believe that there should be less government control and that people should make their own provisions for healthcare. Some individualists criticise the fact that everyone must pay for the NHS through taxation regardless of whether they use it or not. The Conservatives have previously proposed allowing patients to 'top up' their NHS care with private provision if they could afford it.

Collectivist critics claim that this promotes inequality: the founding principle of the NHS was that everyone had equal access to treatment regardless of ability to pay. If private health providers became more involved in the NHS, they would 'cherry-pick' the richest patients and a 'two-tier' system would result, with the oldest, poorest and sickest being left to an overstretched NHS.

Case study 2: Individualist and collectivist views of welfare reform

As welfare states have become a feature of modern western societies, some individualist thinkers have argued that government hand-outs are too generous and encourage people to be lazy and selfish. They argue that people should be more self-reliant. Hard-working families should not pay taxes for the lazy to sit about all day. They also point out that unemployment has become an **intergenerational problem** in cities such as Glasgow and Liverpool and that, in some cases, it is not financially worthwhile to take a job as more money is available on benefits, often supplemented with unofficial earnings. The solution, according to individualists, is **welfare reform**. This would involve drastically cutting benefits to make work more attractive, or forcing claimants to undertake some socially useful work, such as gardening or street-sweeping. This approach was undertaken in the USA and had the effect of significantly reducing the number of welfare recipients.

Collectivists would point to the 'heartlessness' of this approach and claim that it would involve a return to the Victorian **workhouse**, where poor and desperate families were humiliated simply because the main breadwinner had lost his job or died. They also argue that it is not in keeping with the founding principles of the welfare state, where the government pledged to look after the most vulnerable members of society from the cradle to the grave. Also, during times of high unemployment, it is not guaranteed that there are enough jobs for people who are denied welfare. Ultimately, collectivists argue, children would suffer for the failings of their parents and society would see a massive increase in poverty.

Top Tip

Even previous Labour Governments have attempted welfare reforms. Labour brought in private companies to find work for the unemployed and Gordon Brown pledged that there would be 'no life on the dole'.

Quick Test 21

1. In what ways do the individual and collective approaches to government differ?
2. Which party broadly represents which approach?
3. What is the 'nudge' approach to social policy?
4. What are the views of individualists and collectivists on:
   • Private healthcare
   • Welfare reforms

The Decision Making Exercise

The Decision Making Exercise (DME) is always based on Study Theme 2: Wealth and Health Inequalities in the United Kingdom, so possible areas that it could be based on are:

- Health Inequalities
- Wealth Inequalities
- Gender Inequalities
- Race Inequalities
- The Welfare State

Paper 2 is 1 hour and 15 minutes long and in total is worth **30 marks**. It is made up of two parts, **Short Evaluating Questions** and a **Report Writing Task**.

What do you have to do?

1. You will have a range of sources to read through and some questions to answer based on the sources. You may be asked to:
   - identify bias
   - draw conclusions
   - make comparisons between points of view
   - support a point of view.

2. Using the sources and your own background knowledge, you will then write your report.

Short evaluating questions

These are worth a total of **10 marks**. It is therefore worth practising these to build the skills required.

The purpose of the evaluating questions is to familiarise yourself with the sources and begin to build up the arguments to use in your DME.

Keep your answers short and to the point. Your answers should be based only on information contained in the sources.

Sources A and B always offer two different views on the topic of the DME. The views are usually from people such as policy experts, government spokespeople, newspaper columnists or charity workers. The rest of the sources consist of charts, tables and graphs of statistics relating to your DME topic.

The evaluating questions require you to study each of the sources carefully. The question will state which sources you should use to answer the question.

Examples of typical short evaluating questions:
- **To what extent** does the evidence **support** the view in source A?
- **To what extent** has the newspaper columnist been **selective in his/her use of facts**?
- **Give evidence for and against the view** of the newspaper columnist.
- Why might the newspaper columnist be accused of **exaggeration**?
- **Contrast the views** of the charity worker and the newspaper columnist on the effects of the reduction in the provision of free school meals.

What should your answer look like?

To get full marks for an evaluating question you must directly **quote the view** from the supplied source A or B and cite evidence from the chart sources to support your answer. For example:

(SQA 2008)

Q *Use **only** source C1(a) and source A.*

Why might Daphne Miller be accused of exaggeration?

A *In Source A, Daphne Miller **is exaggerating** when she claims 'Free prescriptions would make a huge difference to whether patients did or did not go to their doctor' as **source C1(b)** shows that just over **10% of people surveyed** would be more likely to go to the doctor and, indeed, it would make no difference to nearly **80% of people** if prescriptions were free.*

(2 marks)

(SQA 2009)

Q *Use **only** Source C2(b) and Source B.*

To what extent does the evidence support the view of Jim Waugh?

A *Jim Waugh (Source B) claims that 'More girls than boys are going into both full time higher/further education and employment'. **Source C2(b)** supports Jim as it shows that only **45% of boys are going into full time further/higher education compared to over 60% of girls**. Therefore more girls than boys are going into full time higher/further education.*

*However, **source C2(b) opposes** Jim's view about employment as more boys than girls are going into employment after leaving school: just under **35% of boys are employed whereas just under 25% of girls are employed**. Therefore, the evidence supports Jim's view that gender inequality is improving only to an extent.*

(3 marks)

To answer the question and gain full marks
- Quote the person from source A or B.
- State which source you are using for the facts.
- Quote figures from the source.
- Give an overall conclusion if asked '*to what extent*'.

Check how many marks each question is worth to get an idea of how many points you will have to make.

Top Tip

You should be able to fully answer the evaluating questions in 15–20 minutes. Take 5–10 minutes of this time to familiarise yourself with the sources, reading the views in source A and B carefully. Take about 10 minutes to write out the answers to the questions.

Preparing to write the report

The report is worth **20 marks**. You will be given a title or job description and the best way to present the report is to **imagine that you actually do this job**. For example, you may be a Government policy researcher and have to decide to support or reject the decision to introduce a higher National Minimum Wage. Alternatively, you could be an advisor to the Health Secretary and have to decide if you support or oppose a proposal to extend free prescriptions for all.

You will be given a **summary** of the decision you must make, and instructions as to who the report is for and to use all sources available along with your own **background knowledge**. Below is an example of how the report instructions are laid out; you should spend a few minutes reading this through to make sure you fully understand what your report will be recommending or rejecting.

DECISION MAKING TASK

You are a social policy researcher. You have been asked to prepare a report for a committee investigating expanding welfare provision in which you recommend or reject the proposal to scrap means-testing for the Education Maintenance Allowance (EMA), making it freely available to all.

Your answer should be written in a style appropriate to a *report*.

Your report should:
- recommend or reject the proposal to scrap means-testing for the Education Maintenance Allowance (EMA) to make it available to all young people over 16 in full time education
- provide arguments to support your decision
- identify and comment on any arguments which may be presented by those who oppose your decision
- refer to all the Sources provided AND
- you **must** include relevant background knowledge.

The written and statistical sources which have been provided are:

SOURCE A: EMA for all will be fairer

SOURCE B: EMA should only be for low income families

SOURCE C: Statistical information

20 marks

The keys to writing a good report are
- making a clear decision
- arguing the points of your decision using the sources to support your points
- including your own background knowledge to further enhance your argument. You must also **balance** your report by providing opposing views to your argument, before counter arguing these opposing views in a **rebuttal**. **You must also use all of the sources available to you in the report**.

Top Tip

You can find past papers online – visit the SQA website at www.sqa.org.uk. Your teacher may also have copies of past papers which you could borrow.

Background knowledge

Top Tip

Background knowledge does not have to be specifically about the DME topic; it can be more general information about health and wealth inequalities in the UK or even other study themes.

You must include your own background knowledge (BK) throughout the report. Since Paper 2 is based on Study Theme 2 (Social Issues in the UK), you will have lots of relevant information you can use as BK. Once you have read the sources, you could spend a few minutes noting down any relevant background knowledge which you may be able to include in your report.

In addition to stating which source your information comes from, highlight to the examiner where you have used background knowledge by putting a 'BK' in the margin or in brackets at the end of a sentence.

Structure of the report

Introduction – state who you are, the date and who the report is being written for. State your decision clearly at the outset.

Arguments for – using the sources and background knowledge to provide points supporting your decision.

Arguments against – using the sources and background knowledge to provide points showing that you recognise opposing points of view.

Rebuttal – a counter-argument to the opposing point of view – or, in simple terms, your reply to the arguments against.

Conclusion – a summing up of your report, recognising that the majority of the evidence goes in favour of your recommendation.

The way to write the report

The report is set out in a very different way from your essays. You should set your report out in a formal style with different sections, headings and subheadings. When you use information, you should say which source it was from. Remember to also highlight background knowledge (BK).

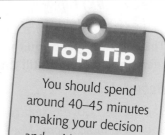

Top Tip

You should spend around 40–45 minutes making your decision and writing the report.

Example of an introduction and recommendation

To: Department for Work and Pensions
From: Kirsty McGrath, Social Policy Researcher
Date:1 August 2010
Re: Education and Maintenance Allowance (EMA)

Introduction

There are many arguments for and against scrapping the Education Maintenance Allowance (EMA). I am going to reject the proposal to stop means-testing the EMA and expand it to all pupils over 16.

Example of a layout integrating background knowledge and using the sources in arguments for and against

You should provide at least three or four arguments to support your decision. Below is an example of how you could lay out two of these arguments.

Arguments for

*Jordan Kelly states in **Source B** that the Education Maintenance allowance is currently available to young people from low-income families in full-time education and I propose it should stay that way. **Source D1** shows that over 39 000 young people in Scotland received EMA in 2010, which encouraged these pupils to stay in education and provided them with the financial support which children from middle-class families already have **(Source B)**. EMA is also currently paid over and above Child Benefit and other benefits such as Income Support **(BK)**. Therefore increasing its availability to all will reinforce traditional wealth inequalities, giving better-off families even more money and maintaining the gap between the rich and the poor.*

*EMA is already a huge financial burden on the Scottish Government. It paid out £35·4 million under the EMA scheme in the academic year 2008–09: £27·5 million in weekly payments and £7·9 million in bonus payments **(Source C2 b)**. The Scottish Government could not financially sustain expanding this allowance. Education is a devolved issue, giving the Scottish Government responsibility for facilitating the EMA in Scotland. However the Scottish Government relies on its funding coming in a block grant from Westminster **(BK)**. Therefore introducing EMA for all would result in cuts in other public services, which have already caused public protests in 2010 **(BK)**.*

Arguments for should be decisive and fully support your recommendation.

You should show understanding of the arguments against your proposal. However, they should not overpower your arguments for it. You should provide around two or three arguments against.

Arguments against

I can understand *the reasons in favour of expanding EMA for all. As Gillian Woods claims in* **Source B***, there are far too many young people who fall into the NEET category from all social backgrounds. Indeed,* **Source C1** *develops this point by highlighting that fewer than half of all young people who leave education at 16 go into full time employment. The high level of unemployment in the UK due to the effects of the recession* **(BK)** *is perhaps a reason to extend the EMA for all. It would give those pupils who are unlikely to find a job an alternative to employment.*

The rebuttal gives you the opportunity to show that, although you understand opposing views, your recommendation is still the right choice to make.

Rebuttal

The Scottish Government could waste millions of pounds by making EMA available for all in order to reduce youth unemployment. Not all pupils who receive the EMA stay on for the full academic year. **Source C2** *highlights that only 68% of those currently claiming EMA complete the full academic year. This suggests that scrapping means-testing and making EMA available for all may cost the Government a great deal of money with very little improvement in the number of pupils completing a full year of education, which would defeat the purpose of having pupils stay on in the first place. I feel the money would be taken away from vital public services, which in turn could result in increased unemployment in Scotland ...*

Your conclusion should recognise the arguments against but state that your decision is the best one.

Conclusion

While the arguments put forward to scrap means-testing the EMA have some merit, I believe the argument for keeping EMA as a means-tested benefit for those young people from lower income families is the most persuasive. In a time of public sector cut-backs, directing more money to high-income families would have a negative effect on other public services. Therefore it would be more beneficial to continue to means-test the EMA.

Top Tip

This is an example of how you could structure some of your arguments in the report. Your report should be longer and more detailed.

Remember, this is only an example of how to lay out your DME. In order to gain top marks you should try to write around three or four 'Arguments for' and two or three 'Arguments against' and 'Rebuttals'.

The Constitution of South Africa

To prepare for the exam you should know about the following:

- **The South African political system**
  The role and powers of the South African Government at national, provincial and local levels.
- **Political issues**
  - Participation and representation.
  - Political parties and support from different groups.
  - Political trends.
- **Social and economic issues**
  - The nature and extent of social and economic inequalities.
  - Demands for change.
  - The effectiveness of government responses and the consequences among and within different racial groups.

Introduction to South Africa

For over 50 years a system of **Apartheid** operated in South Africa. The people's rights and freedoms were determined by ethnic background. This meant whites had a lot of power and wealth, while blacks were poor and often mistreated by the Government and the police force.

Apartheid finally ended in 1994 and South Africa became a **constitutional democracy**. The **Constitution** set out the rights and responsibilities of the citizens and politicians. The Constitution recognised the injustice of the Apartheid era and its aim is to create:

'... a democratic and open society in which government is based on the will of the people and every citizen is equally protected by law.' (South African Constitution 1996)

South Africa has **three levels of government: national, provincial and local**. Each level of government is separate according to the Constitution; however, they can co-operate and work together on different matters.

The National Government of South Africa

The Government is made up of three tiers: **the legislature**, **the executive** and **the judiciary**.

Parliament (the legislature)

The national Parliament is based in Cape Town and is **bicameral**; this means it consists of two Houses – the **National Assembly** and the **National Council of Provinces**. It is responsible for making laws relating to all of South Africa.

Top Tip

The Constitution of South Africa can be changed, but it requires a **two-thirds majority** in both Houses.

	THE NATIONAL ASSEMBLY	THE NATIONAL COUNCIL OF PROVINCES
House	Lower	Upper
Representatives	Maximum of 400 Members of Parliament	90 representatives – ten from each of the nine provinces
Elections	Held every five years – a system of Proportional Representation (PR) is used to elect MPs	Held every five years – PR is used to elect the provincial governments
Functions	Elects the President Passes laws Debates Government policy	Represents the interests of the provinces Involved in passing laws

The President (the executive)

The **President** is elected by the National Assembly and is the **head of the national Government**.

The President:

Jacob Zuma, President since May 2009

- can serve a **maximum of two five-year terms**
- is responsible for **appointing the Deputy President**
- is responsible for **appointing the Cabinet** to run the country. For example a Cabinet Minister is responsible for important areas such as health or education.

The Constitutional Court (the judiciary)

The **Constitutional Court is the highest court** in South Africa. The role of the Court is to ensure that laws **do not break the rules of the Constitution**.

The Constitutional Court:

- has **11** judges
- the judges are **independent** and cannot be members of Parliament, the Government or political parties
- the judges are **appointed by the President** after discussions with party political leaders in the National Assembly
- decisions made by the court have to be **followed by all parts of the Government**.

Provincial Government in South Africa

Although, according to the Constitution, each level of government is separate, **the provinces do share power with the National Government over services** such as education, health and housing. All provinces, for instance Western Cape, have complete control over services such as planning, recreation and roads.

Elections for provincial government are held every five years at the same time as the National Assembly election. **Each province is represented by between 30 to 80 representatives**. For example, the most populated province, Gauteng, has more representatives than Northern Cape, the least populated province.

After the elections a **provincial government** is formed. This is headed by a **Premier** who can serve, like the President of South Africa, **a maximum of two five-year terms**. The Premier is responsible for appointing an **Executive Council** (similar to Cabinet).

Quick Test 22

1. Describe the structure of the national Government.
2. Describe the key powers of the President.
3. Describe the structure and the role of the Constitutional Court.
4. Describe in which areas the national Government and provincial Government work together.

South African political parties

Multi-party democracy

South Africa has an **active multi-party political system**, which means the electorate has a great deal of **choice**. There are **over a dozen political parties** represented in Parliament but this has a number of drawbacks. Firstly, having so many political parties means that the vote is often split and **no real and effective opposition to the African National Congress (ANC) has emerged**.

Secondly, since the end of Apartheid in 1994, South African politics has been **dominated by the ANC**. Some people have argued that the country is really a **one-party state**. However, the role of the opposition parties in recent years has increased, **particularly the Democratic Alliance**.

The African National Congress (ANC)

The **ANC dominates politics** in South Africa, gaining **over 60% of the vote** in every election since 1994, and is the present party of government. It currently has **264 seats** in the National Assembly. Its support comes mainly from the majority black population. In 2005, the National Party (which promoted Apartheid) was disbanded. However, many of its supporters have voted ANC, so the party has support from all ethnic groups. **The main aim of the ANC is to deal with the socioeconomic inequalities** that developed under Apartheid. It has attempted to do this through various programmes such as the **no-fee status of schools**, the **Housing Subsidy Scheme** and the **New Growth Path**.

The current South African President is **Jacob Zuma**, who was elected in 2009. Previously, he had been appointed as Deputy President by Thabo Mbeki. In 2006 President Mbeki sacked Zuma due to a corruption scandal but in 2007 Zuma was victorious over Mbeki in the battle to become the next ANC leader. The leadership battle was bitter and Mbeki was forced to resign early, in 2008, by the National Executive Committee of the ANC. The biggest challenge for the ANC, is that of **internal divisions**.

The Democratic Alliance (DA)

The only political party that is likely to be able to **challenge the dominance of the ANC in the foreseeable future is the Democratic Alliance**. In recent elections the DA has sought to **highlight the failure of the ANC Government** to deliver on its election commitments. This approach has clearly been successful, for instance in **2004 the DA only had 47** representatives in the National Assembly, but it increased significantly to **67 in 2009**.

This success is also replicated in elections to the provinces as the DA is the only opposition party to have **won seats in all nine provinces**. In the 2009 election the DA secured a **majority of votes in the province of Western Cape** and **leads the coalition government**.

The DA is currently led by **Helen Zille**. The DA is considered to be **the non-racial alternative to the ANC** and Zille has emphasised that it is a **'party for all the people'**. This message appeared to work as their **share of the vote increased from 2 million in 2004 to 3 million in 2009**. Zille has acknowledged the key to future election success for the DA is to win greater support in the black community.

The Congress of the People (COPE)

The Congress of the People was founded in 2008 by former high-ranking members of the ANC. They **split from the ANC** due to the corruption allegations that Zuma faced and the forced resignation of Mbeki as leader of the ANC and President.

The party, which is led by **Mosiuoa Lekota**, won **30 seats in the National Assembly** in the 2009 election. During the election campaign it positioned itself as a **progressive party** that would reach out to **minorities and women**. Its policies focused on dealing with a number of economic and social problems, such as **crime, poverty and unemployment**.

Top Tip

The Democratic Alliance recently merged with a smaller political party, the Independent Democrats. The DA and COPE are currently discussing **a possible merger** in time for the 2014 election.

The Inkatha Freedom Party (IFP)

The **fourth largest political party** in South Africa is the Inkatha Freedom Party. The majority of its support is drawn from one tribal group, **the Zulus**. Support for IFP has **steadily declined**: since 1994 it has more than halved. This has led some commentators to suggest that it is **'just about finished'**. Despite this it still managed to win **18 seats in the National Assembly in 2009** and it is still an important political force in the province of KwaZulu Natal.

The current party leader is Chief Buthelezi. The IFP has consistently **highlighted ANC dominance and corruption** as its key concerns. They also want to address a range of economic and social problems, for instance **the AIDS crisis, crime, poverty and unemployment**. They believe people need **'a hand up, not a hand down'**. Another area of reform they seek is in how the Government is organised: they believe **provincial government should have more power**. If such reform were to happen, the IFP would gain more power in KwaZulu Natal province.

Pressure Groups in South Africa

Since the end of Apartheid in 1994 pressure groups have campaigned for and promoted a range of causes and interests. Two of the key pressure groups are the **Congress of South Africa Trade Unions** (COSATU) and the **South African National Civic Organisation** (SANCO).

COSATU is a major force in the country and has taken industrial action over the slow pace of social and economic reform to help workers. SANCO's main goals are to improve living conditions for all in South Africa and to end poverty. SANCO is a very **large pressure group with nearly 6 million members**.

One of the main criticisms of pressure groups is that they are **closely linked to the ANC**. The **Tripartite Alliance** is a formal grouping of the ANC, COSATU and the South African Communist Party (SACP). It has led to claims that the ANC has **undemocratic tendencies** and is suspicious of pressure groups that are not loyal to the ANC.

Top Tip

Although the Democratic Alliance is the **main opposition** to the ANC, it **does not have enough support to threaten the dominance** of the ANC.

Quick Test 23

1. To what extent can it be claimed that South Africa is a one-party state?
2. Describe the main political opposition faced by the South African Government.
3. Name three political parties in South Africa and describe what they aim to achieve.
4. Describe why the relationship between pressure groups in South African politics and the ANC has been criticised.

National and provincial election results

In 1994 the first non-race-based elections took place in South Africa. Since then, every South African government has been **dominated by the African National Congress** (ANC). ANC support is drawn from the **majority black population** – largely because many believe the ANC conquered Apartheid.

Despite increased dissatisfaction with the pace of social and economic change made by the ANC, the party **dominates at every level of government** – National, Provincial and Municipal. In the 2009 National Assembly election, the ANC won **65·9%** of the vote; only slightly down on the 66·3% of the vote they won in the municipal elections in 2006.

Top Tip

In the May 2011 municipal elections support for the ANC fell to 62% – the **lowest ever vote share for the ANC. Support for DA increased significantly** to 24% but this still does not challenge the dominance of the ANC. Because of such high support for the ANC, many people question how democratic South Africa is in reality. And in 2009 President Zuma made a very powerful claim – that the ANC would remain in power 'until Jesus comes back'.

2009 Election Results

National Assembly

POLITICAL PARTY	PERCENTAGE OF THE VOTE	ASSEMBLY SEATS
African National Congress	65·9%	264
Democratic Alliance	16·7%	67
Congress of the People	7·4%	30
Inkatha Freedom Party	4·5%	18
Eight other parties	5·5%	21
Electoral turnout	***77·3%***	

2009 saw a slight increase in electoral turnout; this was partly due to changes in voting laws and partly because many people were unhappy with the speed of change under the ANC. Furthermore, 2009 was the **first National Assembly** in which the ANC **did not have the two-thirds majority** that is required to change the Constitution, i.e. 264 seats rather than the 267 required.

Provincial elections

In 2009, the ANC continued to dominate South African politics by winning control of eight provinces. However, the DA has made significant political progress in one province, Western Cape. **The DA won the majority of the votes and is part of a Coalition Government in Western Cape**.

Despite this minor defeat, the strength of the ANC is demonstrated throughout the rest of the country: the highest vote share was in Mpumalanga with **86%** of the vote; the second lowest vote share was in Northern Cape with **60·7%** of the vote. This means it will be some time before the DA can challenge the ANC in other provinces.

The National Assembly and provincial election results have continued to show that the ANC is the **most powerful political party** in South Africa.

2004 election results

National Assembly

2004 saw a **decline** in electoral turnout, due to dissatisfaction with the ANC's social and economic policies. Despite the decline in turnout, **the ANC increased their number of seats** in the National Assembly from 266 in 1999 to **279 in 2004**, a two-thirds majority in the National Assembly.

POLITICAL PARTY	PERCENTAGE OF THE VOTE	ASSEMBLY SEATS
African National Congress	69·7%	279
Democratic Alliance	12·4%	50
Inkatha Freedom Party	7·0%	28
United Democratic	2·3%	9
Eight other parties	8·6%	34
Electoral turnout	*76·7%*	

Provincial elections

In 2004, similar to 2009, the ANC was the party of government – for instance they won outright **control of seven provinces**. In the other two provinces they shared power with the **Democratic Alliance** and the **Inkatha Freedom Party**. In the provinces the ANC did not win outright, they managed to gain **45% to 48%** of the total vote.

Both election results show that the ANC continue to be the **strongest political party in South Africa**, as yet not significantly challenged in the post-Apartheid era.

Dominance of the ANC

The ANC has dominated all elections since 1994. It has strong support throughout the provinces and has a key role within the trade union movement with its alliance with COSATU. For these reasons, **it is claimed by some that South Africa is a one-party state**.

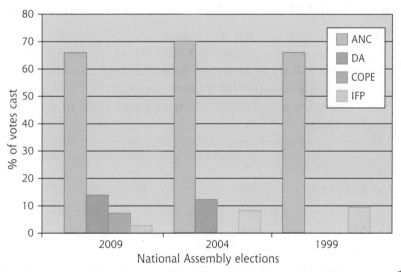

Quick Test 24

1. What evidence is there that the ANC has support throughout South Africa?
2. Explain why the ANC is the dominant political party.
3. For what reasons was there an increase in electoral turnout in 2009?
4. Give reasons to support and oppose the view that South Africa is a 'healthy democracy'.

Economic and social inequalities

Many South Africans suffered greatly during the Apartheid era of 1948 to 1994. Despite becoming a democracy in 1994 many experts claim that the **legacy of Apartheid** has caused the majority of economic and social inequalities experienced by South Africans today.

Employment and unemployment

South Africa is viewed as the **economic powerhouse of the continent of Africa**. This view is supported by economists who believe the country will be one of the world's fastest growing economies over the next three decades. However, **unemployment is very high** – according to the Government, **the official rate is 25%**. This figure is disputed and it is argued that **the true level of unemployment is nearer 40%**.

Since the end of Apartheid **black South Africans have experienced the largest increase in employment**; for example, in 1994 only 43% were employed but by 2008 it was 53%. However, this is still lower than coloured and Indian South Africans who have higher employment rates of 57% and 61% respectively. **White South Africans have the highest employment rate at 64%.**

Black South Africans do less well in education than any other ethnic group. The impact of this is that although more black South Africans are in employment, they are **more likely to be in low paid jobs than any other ethnic group**. Furthermore, **black people are more likely to suffer from unemployment**. This is important because there is **no welfare state** in South Africa. The overall result is extremely **high rates of poverty at 60% for blacks compared to only 3% for whites**.

Top Tip

The **New Growth Path**, a Government policy to create millions of new jobs, is **focused on improving education**. The Government believes better education will help **create good jobs** and **reduce unemployment and poverty**.

Crime

In 2007 the South African Government asked a group of academics to carry out research into why there is such a **high crime rate**. The research concluded that it can be linked to a range of economic and social factors: **high unemployment, poverty, the absence of a stable family life and alcohol and drug abuse**. Before hosting the World Cup in 2010 the country was bottom of an international crime survey with **50 murders, 100 rapes, 500 violent assaults and 700 burglaries occurring every day**.

Critics of the ANC Government claim the high rate of crime is linked to **police corruption and lack of funding for the police and criminal justice system**. The corruption would appear to reach the very top. At the end of 2011, **Jackie Selebi**, the former chief of the South African Police Service, was imprisoned for helping the Mafia.

The high rate of crime leads to two main responses – the **poor live in fear** and the **rich spend money on security**. In the townships, for instance Soweto, the police have struggled to establish law and order. The people in such areas take the law into their own hands and **dispense rough justice**. The South African Government has quadrupled spending on law and order since the mid-1990s, but this is a small increase when compared to the money spent by the rich on private security. There are now over 300 000 security guards protecting the richest communities in South Africa.

Education

Education is often viewed as the key to addressing a range of social and economic problems, for example crime and poverty. Recent research has highlighted that young people who achieve the basic school leaving certificate are less likely to commit crime than those who do not. The Government has **doubled spending on education** since the end of Apartheid.

Education is **compulsory** for all children aged 7 to 15 years. In addition nearly 90% of six year olds are enrolled in school. However, schooling is not free for all and has resulted in a **two-tier system of education**. Due to school fees, the system favours wealthy parents over poor parents. The impact is that many children do not finish high school and those who do are predominately white; **nearly 70% of whites** have a high school qualification compared to **less than 20% of blacks**. The lack of basic qualifications limits future employment opportunities. The consequence is that blacks are more likely to be caught in a **cycle of poverty** that means they live in substandard and poorer quality housing.

Housing

The South African Constitution has stated that everyone '… has a right to have access to adequate housing.' Although this is a right, **15% of the population live in shanty towns**. According to 2007 Government figures 80% of households now have access to electricity and 88% have access to clean water. Despite this progress – for example, **1·2 million new houses have been built since 2004** – the Housing Development Agency says **another 1·5 million houses need to be built by 2014** to meet the Government target of eradicating poor quality housing.

Health

There are stark inequalities in the provision of healthcare. The majority of people use basic healthcare which is offered free by the Government. However, this is underfunded and overstretched. **80% of the population, mainly black, rely on free healthcare**. Standards of healthcare vary across the country, with poorer provinces such as Eastern Cape facing greater health problems than wealthier provinces like Western Cape.

According to the World Health Organisation (WHO), in 2005 **South Africa spent nearly 9% of its GNP** (the amount of wealth produced by a country) on healthcare. The majority of this spending (60%) was on private healthcare. This system favours the richest people in South Africa as the private sector only provides care for 20% of the population.

The South African Government announced in 2010 that it would establish a **National Health Insurance** system based on the principles of universal coverage and access to healthcare based on need and not on ability to pay. As part of this, the Health Minister has said there needs to be a move towards primary healthcare – that is clinics such as doctors' surgeries rather than hospitals.

The HIV/AIDS epidemic is on such a huge scale in South Africa that resources are diverted from dealing with other health concerns such as tuberculosis and malaria. It is estimated that there are **5·6 million people** in the country with the illness. A significant number are children, with almost one in four babies in South Africa testing positive for HIV. According to the United Nations **310 000 South Africans died from AIDS in 2009**. That is **850 people per day**.

Quick Test 25

1. Explain why crime is a major problem in South Africa.
2. Explain why access to education and healthcare is still an issue in South Africa.
3. Describe the extent of the HIV/AIDS epidemic in South Africa.
4. Explain the impact that lack of educational success has on other social and economic problems.

South African Government policies

Education and literacy

Education spending has grown by 14% a year over the last three years and remains the Government's largest area of expenditure. The Government is committed to **improving literacy and numeracy** with workbooks being made available in **all 11 official languages**. It has also **expanded the number of mobile libraries throughout the country**. In addition, all learners are tested at grades three, six and nine.

The Government is focused on improving access to education for the poorest in the country through the **no-fee status of schools** (the Government pays the fees for the poorest children); this has been increased from **40% to 60% of schools**. The Government has aimed to improve the quality of education through the **Teacher Laptop Initiative** introduced in 2009, whereby every teacher will be issued with a laptop paid through a monthly allowance.

Due to the legacy of Apartheid many people opted out of education and in 2008 the **Kha Ri Gude** (Let us learn) mass literacy campaign was launched. This has committed the Government to spend R6·1 billion over five years to halve South Africa's illiteracy rates by 2015.

The Reconstruction and Development Programme (RDP)

RDP was introduced in the aftermath of Apartheid and its aim was to provide **'an improved standard of living and quality of life for all South Africans within a peaceful and stable society'**. The main criticism of RDP was its failure to deliver adequate improvements quickly enough. There are many examples of this, for instance in housing and healthcare. One aim was to **build 1 million new homes within five years**. It actually took ten years and many of the houses built were substandard. Access to healthcare was greatly expanded for 5 million people through 500 new clinics. However, despite this, average life expectancy declined from 64 years to 53 years.

Growth, Employment and Redistribution (GEAR)

GEAR replaced the RDP in the late 1990s with the aim of strengthening the economy. Economic growth had stagnated during the Apartheid era and it was believed that the Government could better provide for the population by helping people to help themselves. This would be achieved by **creating jobs, reducing poverty and privatising (selling) state assets**. The overall success of GEAR was limited: the economy did become more stable but it did not create as many jobs as planned. It also had a limited impact on wealth distribution, with wealth still being unevenly distributed along racial lines.

Top Tip

When you are writing about policies that deal with social and economic inequalities, you should **evaluate how successful they have been**.

Affirmative Action

The **Employment Equity Act 1998** introduced the Affirmative Action programme. This is a controversial programme, as many people believe it is unconstitutional.

The aim of the programme is to **redress hundreds of years of discrimination** against blacks, mixed race and Asian people in South Africa.

Affirmative Action is also referred to as **positive discrimination**, which means companies have to **discriminate in favour** of the black majority, as well as minority groups such as coloured people and the disabled. This law allows non-whites access to a range of jobs, for example in the public sector within Government, the Civil Service and the police, and in the private sector. They are offered jobs at every level in the public sector, from junior positions to senior management positions. Private companies that employ **over 50 employees** must reflect the population make-up or they can be fined. However, companies that employ a significant number of non-whites in management positions are **offered favourable treatment and guaranteed federal contracts**.

Black Economic Empowerment

The Black Economic Empowerment (BEE) Act of 2004 was introduced to support the continued **development of black economic entrepreneurship**. The aim of the law was to create a more equitable society and its supporters have argued that it is the best way to deal with racial inequalities. However, critics have argued that the South African Government's commitment is not focused on meeting the socioeconomic needs of all groups in the country.

Top Tip

It is important to **stay up to date** with policies that deal with social and economic inequalities. You should do this by checking quality newspapers and the internet regularly.

The aim was to ensure that the **non-white majority have a share of the socioeconomic power that reflects their share of the population**. Companies have to meet three requirements in the BEE legislation:
* Provide suitable staff development and training
* Purchase some materials from firms which follow BEE legislation
* Have a number of blacks in senior and middle management posts.

The New Growth Path

The Government introduced the New Growth Path in 2010 to address, according to the Deputy President, **Kgalema Motlanthe**, '... the deep inequalities left by Apartheid'. The aim is to create **5 million new jobs by 2020** and therefore reduce official unemployment from 25% to 15%. The Government has set out six areas for job creation and growth: agriculture, the 'green' economy, infrastructure, manufacturing, mining and tourism.

The Government has recognised that the success of NGP depends on Government, businesses and civil society working together. However, groups like COSATU have highlighted the limited role for the public sector and argued that the role of education and healthcare should be expanded.

The main targets of the NGP include:
* Improving education and skills training
* Producing more engineers
* Promoting and supporting small businesses
* Developing more export opportunities for South African companies.

Quick Test 26

1. Which policies have the South African Government introduced to improve standards of education throughout the country?

2. For what reasons was the RDP replaced by GEAR?

3. Explain what is meant by Affirmative Action and give at least two examples of this policy.

4. Describe the aim of the BEE policy introduced in 2004.

Successes and limitations of Government policies

Education

The Government has attempted to deal with the legacy of Apartheid through the **Kha Ri Gude literacy campaign**. This programme has had some success as, by 2009, an **additional 620 000 people were literate**. However, this is **far short of the 4·7 million literacy target** for 2015.

The Government has sought to improve compulsory education through the **Teacher Laptop Initiative**, the **National School Nutrition Programme** and the **no-fee status of schools**.

The full benefits of these programmes are yet to be seen and concerns remain about the quality of teaching. However, the National School Nutrition Programme has been successful in feeding 5·6 million children per school day. This has led to improvements in health and examination passes. The no-fee status of schools programme was extended from 40% to 60% of the poorest schools in 2010.

> **Top Tip**
>
> The key to dealing with social and economic problems is through **education**. Improvements in education, for black South Africans in particular, are likely to lead to improvements in pay, health and housing, and a reduction in crime.

Unemployment and employment

The 2010 Football World Cup in South Africa produced many benefits. For example, it **accelerated improvements to infrastructure** in the country with new roads and improved airports. It is estimated that the tournament **created 300 000 jobs** and **resulted in increased economic activity of at least R18 billion**.

Unemployment has a disproportionate impact upon black South Africans and there is a **'lost generation'** who received little or no education during Apartheid. Black, coloured and Indian/Asian South Africans have higher levels of unemployment than whites. For example, in 2010, the **unemployment rate for blacks was nearly 30% compared to 6% for whites**. Furthermore, there are significant pay differences – in 2008 the average **annual salary of whites was R135 000 compared to that of blacks at R19 500**. Differences in unemployment and income levels highlight the limitations of the Employment Equity Act and the Black Economic Empowerment Act.

However, at the end of 2010, the Government introduced a new programme to encourage economic growth – the **Framework of the New Economic Growth Path**. The aim is to create 5 million new jobs over the next ten years. This, it is acknowledged, will be difficult due to the impact of the credit crunch and global economic downturn.

Health

The Government has expanded healthcare throughout the country, for example by **building 3000 new clinics in rural areas**. In addition **free healthcare**, made available to **children under six and pregnant women**, has improved mortality and morbidity rates. The under-five mortality rate was 73 per 1000 births in 2000 but by 2011 it had dropped to 43. Despite such programmes, **life expectancy has continued to fall from 61 in 1990 to 49 in 2011**.

The **Expanded Programme on Immunisation** has played a role in reducing child mortality rates, providing vaccinations against preventable diseases such as measles. There has been progress with 78% of children immunised in 2002; by 2008 this had reached 85%. However, this is short of the 90% target set for 2008.

The most significant healthcare challenge facing South Africa is the **HIV/AIDS epidemic**. South Africa has the highest HIV/AIDS rate in the world – there are an estimated **850 deaths per day due to the illness**. Such high rates of infection and morbidity have weakened the economy, as many young professionals have lost their lives and children have lost their parents. Up until recently, the South African Government had failed to acknowledge the extent of the problem and denied treatment to HIV/AIDS sufferers due to cost. In 2008 the Constitutional Court ruled that sufferers should have access to antiretroviral drugs. Political attitudes have changed with a **target to reduce the spread of the disease by 50% by 2011**.

Housing

The Government introduced the **Housing Subsidy Scheme** and the **Community Residential Units Programme** (CRUP) to deal with high rents. The HSS income level has not changed from R3500 per month or less in over a decade, meaning that people have to be poorer in real terms today to qualify for the scheme. CRUP-supported households who cannot afford housing are offered converted hostel accommodation as secure properties to rent.

The standard of housing has shown limited improvement. In 2004, former President Mbeki pledged that all houses would have access to running water within five years. However, by 2011, **only 88% of people had access to running water**. The current Government aims to provide all citizens with access to running water and basic sanitation by 2014. This will be a significant challenge as it is estimated that 5 to 15 million people still live in **shanty towns**.

Redistribution of land is an important policy which aims to transfer land back into the hands of blacks who were forced off the land. Progress has been slow. The current Government target is to transfer 30% of land previously owned by whites to blacks by 2015. However, by 2008, only 5% had been transferred; this is due to the resistance of white farmers, the difficulty of proving land claims and the high compensation costs involved.

Crime

Crime has been a major problem in South Africa. However, the investment in the World Cup in 2010 played a positive role, contributing to a massive 90% drop in crime.

The high levels of crime are partly a legacy of Apartheid and partly due to the wealth gap in the country. People with a high standards of living may feel more secure living in gated communities with private security.

The Government has attempted to reduce crime by recruiting more blacks into the police force. It hopes that they will act as positive role models for young people trapped in poverty who might turn to crime. **Between 2004 and 2010 the number of police increased by 60 000** but the South African Police Service has said it cannot reduce crime alone. They say that crime can only be reduced through addressing social and economic problems.

Quick Test 27

1. Describe the impact of hosting the Football World Cup in 2010 on at least two social and economic problems.
2. Explain the policies introduced by the South African Government to help the poorest people in the country.
3. Explain the impact of the HIV/AIDS epidemic on the social and economic development of South Africa.
4. How successfully has the South African Government tackled inequalities in education, housing and health?

Background information

To prepare for the exam you should know about the following:

- **The Chinese political system and political issues**
    - The role and power of the Chinese Government at national, regional and local levels
    - The role of the Chinese Communist Party and the extent of its political opposition
    - The participation and representation of Chinese people.
- **Social and economic issues**
    - The nature and extent of social and economic inequalities and change.
    - The effectiveness of government responses and the consequences for people in China.
- **Human rights in China**
    - Groups facing inequality and the extent to which Chinese citizens have freedom of expression.

> **Top Tip**
>
> China has one of the fastest growing economies in the world. China has the second largest economy in the world, next to the USA, and is predicted to become the largest economy in the world by 2020.

China statistics

- Population 1 330 141 295
- Capital: Beijing
- President: Hu Jintao
- Sex ratios:
    - at birth: 1·14 male(s)/female
    - under 15 years: 1·17 male(s)/female
    - 15–64 years: 1·06 male(s)/female
    - 65 years and over: 0·93 male(s)/female
    - total population: 1·06 male(s)/female (2010 est.)
- Life expectancy at birth:
    - total population: 74·51 years
    - male: 72·54 years
    - female: 76·77 years (2010 estimate)
- GNI per capita US $3620

China

China is the most populated country in the world, with over 1·3 billion people living there. It is the fourth largest country in the world and is 120 times bigger than Scotland. China makes up 20% of the world's population, therefore one in five people in the world is Chinese.

China has transformed its economy since the 1970s from a **state-controlled closed economy**, in which the Government owned and controlled all companies, to a new **market economy** that is reliant on trade with other countries. China is now a major player in the global market.

Westernisation

China has an increasingly westernised lifestyle. Rising incomes have created a bigger demand for western fashion, cars and fast food, as well as movies and sport on satellite TV. In 2010 China had over 900 branches of McDonald's and 2000 KFCs. Between 2004 and 2010 the number of internet users went from 94 million to over 420 million! New car registrations have trebled and 80% of people in urban areas own their own homes.

However, not all parts of China have benefited from these changes. There is inequality between rural and urban areas and a widening gap between the rich and the poor.

Comparing the rural province of Gansu with the urban province of Guangdong highlights this inequality.

COMPARISON OF GANSU AND GUANGDONG		
	Gansu	**Guangdong**
Population	26 million; 73% rural	93 million; 34% migrants
Life expectancy	67 years	73 years
Literacy	75%	91%
Industries	mining, electricity generation, petrochemicals, tobacco	electrical goods, garments, toys, shoes, construction
Agriculture	42% of land area is mountain and desert; main crops: grain, vegetables, melons, medicinal herbs	10% of land area intensively cultivated; main crops: rice, livestock, tea, tropical fruits
GDP	£15·8 billion	£180·4 billion
Disposable income	£562 urban; £136 rural	£1026 urban; £326 rural
Foreign investment	£9·8 million	£6 billion - Special Enterprise Zone
Imports	£739 million	£94 billion
Exports	£542 million	£117 billion

Economic developments

Iron rice bowl

The iron rice bowl is an expression which refers to an employment programme started by the Chinese Communist Government in the 1950s. The programme guaranteed job security for life for employees of state-run businesses and also provided food, education, healthcare and housing. This guarantee had obvious benefits but it also created problems: with guaranteed job security it didn't matter if you were good at your job or liked what you did – it was very hard to get fired for incompetence.

Market economy

China was traditionally a **closed economy** whereby the Communist Government owned and controlled all businesses and industries. However, since the 1970s, China has changed the way it runs its economy and now has an open door policy with the rest of the world.

The traditional state-owned economy was failing to meet the needs of the growing population in China, with a large number of people living in poverty. In 1981 it was estimated that over half of the population was living in poverty.

The economy was put through a number of progressive reforms. In 1978–79 China witnessed the end of the iron rice bowl when Deng Xiaoping introduced the **Household Responsibility System**. This reform allowed farmers to grow and sell surplus food on the open market and removed restrictions on what they were allowed to produce. Rules for the production industry were also relaxed, allowing factories to produce goods to supply market demand, rather than to meet government quotas.

Many **State Owned Enterprises** (SOEs) were inefficient and failed to produce profits. Under the iron rice bowl, millions of Chinese citizens relied on SOEs for employment and social support, such as housing and healthcare. However, as a result of their inefficiency, many state owned enterprises closed down after the introduction of the economic reforms causing high levels of unemployment and poverty.

Foreign trade and investment in China

In 1992 Deng Xiaoping introduced **Special Economic Zones** (SEZs) to open up China to the world and encourage foreign businesses to invest in China. SEZs were set up around coastal areas of China to make it easier to export goods produced there. Businesses setting up inside SEZs enjoyed tax incentives and cheap labour, encouraging the economy to boom. The main business sectors that invested in SEZs were banking, technology industries, electronic manufacturing and textiles.

China marked the 30th anniversary of its first special economic zone, Shenzhen, in September 2010. From a small fishing village in south China's Guangdong province, Shenzhen has now developed into a booming metropolis, home to a number of high-tech firms and manufacturing industries.

In 2001 China joined the World Trade Organisation (WTO). This resulted in foreign trade doubling in China, and allowed Chinese companies to invest abroad and many more foreign companies to invest in China. These companies range from banking and the finance industry to manufacturing and service industries. China has been nicknamed the 'workshop of the world'. It manufactures two-thirds of the world's microwave ovens, DVD players, shoes and toys.

Top Tip

China trade facts: Many huge multinational companies have set up in China. Starbucks, for example, now has over 400 coffee bars in China and IKEA has Chinese stores. Walmart, the biggest corporation in the world, is the largest importer of Chinese products to the United States.

Migration

China has experienced the largest migration within a country in history; the people moving around the country for work are known as the '**floating population**' of migrant workers. An estimated 100 million rural residents have left the countryside in search of employment in the big cities over the last decade. Migrant workers provide cheap labour for both multinational companies and state-owned enterprises in China. Migrant workers, desperate for employment, often work very long hours in factories for very little pay. Many factories will provide basic food and accommodation for their workers. As a result of the low pay these migrant workers receive, factories and businesses can make huge profits on their products.

Hukou permit system

This is a record system that officially registers where people live and other personal data. The system has been relaxed in some provinces in recent years. For example, Guangdong province cancelled the system in 2010 and replaced it with a residence permit system. This means that migrant workers in Guangdong can now enjoy more benefits, such as free vaccinations for children and some social security benefits. However, such changes are not uniform across China. In Beijing, the Hukou restrictions are still strict. Migrant workers in Beijing face charges for healthcare and secondary education, and have no access to social security.

Shenzhen City's skyline

Quick Test 28

1. Describe the transformation of China from a state-controlled economic system to a market economy.
2. Explain how the Household Responsibility System has helped rural farmers enjoy economic development.
3. In what ways have the SEZs, foreign investment and trade in China helped China's economic growth?
4. Explain why migrant workers are an important part of China's growing economy.

Social and economic inequalities

China's economic reforms have improved the lives of millions of Chinese citizens. They have opened up job opportunities both in China and the rest of the world. However, these reforms have also highlighted the huge inequalities faced by the people of China.

Wealth

The Office of Economic Co-operation and Development (OECD) reported in 2010 that China is now leading the world economy out of recession. Already the world's second largest economy, China could well overtake the United States to become the leading producer of manufactured goods in the next five to seven years.

Despite its large economy, there **are massive wealth inequalities in China**. Inequalities are most evident when looking at the differences between people living in urban and rural areas. A report which looked at world wealth (the 2010 Credit Suisse Global Wealth Report) highlighted that people in rural countryside areas in China were much more likely to be poor than people from urban towns and cities. The report showed that in 2010, people from rural countryside areas in China had an annual average per capita disposable income of 5900 yuan (roughly £590). This was much less than the income of people from urban towns and cities in China, where the average annual per capita disposable income was 19 100 yuan (roughly £1930). **This shows that there is a massive gap between the rich and the poor in China, and that the wealth in China is unevenly distributed between urban and rural areas.**

(Source BBC News http://www.bbc.co.uk/news/business-13945072)

Urban China has 108 billionaires, the second-highest number of billionaires per country (only the USA has more.) However, rural areas, home to two-thirds of Chinese citizens, have not received the benefits of China's economic growth. Although poverty has been reduced, **160 million** Chinese people continue to live on **under US $1 per day**, and **486 million live on $2 per day**. It is estimated that 16% of the population of China live below the international poverty line of $1·25 per day.

In 2009 **urban** per-capita income stood at 17175 yuan ($2500), more than three times the average **rural** income of 5153 yuan, highlighting the massive urban/rural divide in wealth.

Education

The Chinese education system states that all children should have nine years of education, which is usually made up of six years of elementary or primary education and three years of junior education. However, this system is beset with inequalities. Children from poorer families often drop out of school due to the costs associated with attending. Families have to pay education fees for books, stationery, uniforms and equipment. This cost increases for those living outside their Hukou permit area. The result of these fees is that children from poorer families and migrant worker families are more likely to drop out of school early. Another factor which contributes to the high drop-out rate in rural areas is the fact that many rural households need their children to work, for example by assisting in the fields, to supplement the family's income. There has, however, been an increase in the number of children attending primary school in recent years, but this has not translated into more graduations from junior secondary schools.

Top Tip

Economic reforms have benefited many people in China but they have also caused a great deal of inequality in education, healthcare, employment and housing.

Therefore, although more children are attending primary school than ever before, many children from rural areas are not able to graduate from junior school.

The gap between urban and rural schools is also highlighted in the qualifications of teachers. In rural areas, it is rare for a junior high school teacher to have attended university – only one in five has done so, compared to three-quarters of teachers in urban areas such as Beijing.

Health

Although China is a Communist country, **healthcare is not free for all** and there is a great deal of **inequality** in the Chinese healthcare system. Individuals often have to rely on private medical insurance to get decent healthcare. China ranked 187th out of 191 countries in a World Health Organisation (WHO) survey measuring the equality of medical treatment. Therefore, according to the WHO, China is one of the most unequal countries in the world in their provision of healthcare.

There are large differences in life expectancy, between the rich urban elite and the urban poor, and between people in rural and urban areas. A farmer in a rural province can expect to live to around 65 years of age whereas in a rich urban province life expectancy can reach 75 years of age.

Corruption is a big problem for the health system; hospitals cannot make much money from the poor, so they often increase prices for richer patients' operations. There is evidence that the poor are avoiding medical help, while the rich are paying more and more for their treatment. Half of doctors' salaries come from drug sales, leading to over-prescribing and reports of unnecessary operations and procedures.

Housing

High rise overcrowded apartments in Hong Kong

There is a big gap between the quality of housing for the rich and the poor in China. While the rich enjoy a housing boom, the poor cannot afford rising house prices. China has experienced a big rise in house prices since the economic reforms, with house prices in some areas rising by 25% each year. The Property Law of 2007 legalised buying and selling homes. People in China are buying homes as a way of saving for the future because they cannot rely on state pensions and other social security benefits. New luxurious housing developments are satisfying the demands of the rich in China; however, the less well-off are struggling to afford mortgages or rent for high-rise housing blocks. It is likely that nearly 200 million rural residents will move into cities over the next few years, creating huge housing demands, so many of these migrants will find themselves living in overcrowded flats with poor sanitation.

The rapid growth of the urban population, due to large-scale migration within China, has put a huge strain on housing and public services such as transport, energy supplies, water and sanitation. This has led to urban sprawl, where cities are expanding into the countryside. Urban sprawl has the potential to cause social unrest as it creates problems between property developers and dispossessed farmers, and between factory bosses and their rural workforce.

Crime

The crime rate in China **tripled between 1984 and 2004**. In 2004, there were more than a million serious crimes. In 2006, there was a rise in the number of major criminal cases, including bombings, kidnappings and homicides, with an increase in the number of crimes being committed by younger people.

The Overseas Security Advisory Council (OSAC) reports that the overall crime threat in China is still relatively low. Nevertheless, petty and violent crime continues to increase, and this has worsened as a result of the worldwide economic crisis. An OSAC report published in 2009 stated that crime had been increasing at a rate of 10% per year since the late 1970s and early 1980s, when the Deng reforms were introduced. It seems that the economic reforms and growth have been accompanied by an increase in petty crime, drug abuse, prostitution, truck-hijacking and kidnapping. The rise in crime rates has been blamed on the breakdown of Mao's Communist ideals of discipline, and the rise of capitalist competition, as well as links between the police and criminal gangs.

Top Tip

The economic reforms introduced by Deng have resulted in a significant rise in both petty crime and organised crime in China.

Large scale unemployment will contribute to this trend, especially in the southern part of the country where dozens of production factories have closed. (The Chinese Academy of Sciences estimates that at least 4 million migrant labourers have been out of work since the end of the Olympics in 2008.)

Organised crime – counterfeiting, money laundering, theft, kidnapping, human smuggling and drug trafficking – is a growing problem in China. This new trend of organised crime has created a huge hidden economy. This is in part due to some Chinese businesses dealing in and profiting from selling counterfeit goods both in China and abroad. The European Commission have criticised this type of organised crime by saying the huge amount of counterfeit goods being imported into the EU is damaging to the European economy. In 2010 it was estimated that over 64% of seized counterfeit cigarettes and fake designer clothing, shoes, toys, CDs and DVDs imported into the EU came from China.

(Source BBC News http://www.bbc.co.uk/news/world-europe-11155110)

Quick Test 29

1. Give evidence to support the view that there is a big difference between the wealth of urban and rural citizens.

2. In what way has the growth in the economy benefited some people in China?

3. Explain what inequalities migrant workers might suffer from due to the Hukou permit system.

4. In what ways are healthcare and education provision not equal for all in China?

5. Explain why crime rates have risen in recent years in China.

6. In what ways have the economic developments in China made people's lives better or worse?

Impact of the 2008 Beijing Olympics

Beijing 2008

On 13 July 2001, the International Olympic Committee announced that Beijing would host the 2008 Olympic Games. This marked a huge change for the people of China, particularly those in Beijing. Many believed that the Olympic Games would give Beijing the opportunity to improve much of its housing and infrastructure; investments that would benefit the people of China long after the games were over. The Olympics was also an event that allowed China to show the world it had transformed into a great economic and political power. Premier Wen Jiabao said the Beijing Olympics presented an opportunity for China to show the world that it is 'democratic, open, civilized, friendly, and harmonious'.

In addition to Beijing, six other cities hosted Olympic events—Hong Kong; Qingdao; Shandong; Qinhuangdao; Hebei; Shanghai; Shenyang, Liaoning; and Tianjin—making the Olympics a national event and bringing improvements to many areas in China. Between 2002 and 2006, China invested nearly $40 billion in infrastructure to prepare for the games. This transformed the cityscape of Beijing.

Social and Economic Benefits from the Olympics

Facilities

A brand new Olympic Park and 37 venues for hosting events were built. These included the state of the art National Stadium or 'birds nest' in Beijing, a sailing centre in Qingdao and football ('soccer') stadiums in Tianjin, Qinhuangdao, Shenyang, and Shanghai.

Transportation and infrastructure

China spent over $1.1 billion on transportation improvements, including building and extending Beijing's subway system, completing the city's light rail system, and constructing and refurbishing more than 318 km of city streets. Residents of Beijing and visitors also benefited from a new airport terminal at the Beijing Capital International Airport.

Urban renewal

In keeping to Beijing's 11th Five-Year Plan (2006–10), Beijing spent more than $200 million demolishing run-down housing and urban buildings, and making extensive refurbishments and improvements to housing areas.

Environmental improvements

Similar to many other big cities in China, Beijing suffers from polluted air and smog. Air quality, particularly in the summer, can be dangerously low. Beijing took steps to improve air quality, including ordering coal-burning power plants to reduce emissions and requesting 200 heavily polluting factories to move out of the city. However, these environmental improvements have not benefited Chinese citizens long-term, as construction projects, traffic restrictions and factory closures were only enforced in the run-up to the Olympics.

Housing

Thousands of houses built to accommodate athletes during the Olympics were sold to residents of Beijing after the Games had ended. Although this provided 'affordable' housing in Beijing, China has been criticised over its handling of the construction of these houses. According to the Centre on Housing Rights and Evictions (COHRE), 1.5 million people were displaced between 2000 and 2008 for the construction of Beijing's Olympics. Most of these people were low-income workers, who were unable to afford the Olympic apartments sold after the Games. There were reports of thousands of forced evictions in Beijing, often without due process or compensation. In a December 2007 report, COHRE estimated that as many as 1.5 million Beijing residents were forced from their homes in the run-up to the 2008 Olympics. The report also states that during the pre-Olympic 'clean-up' of Beijing, there were forced closures of dozens of schools for children of migrant workers.

Government responses

China's premier **Wen Jiabao** opened China's annual parliamentary session by promising to tackle a growing social divide and make 'improving people's well-being' the focus of the country's development.

At the start of the **National People's Congress** (NPC) in Beijing in March 2010, Wen Jiabao admitted that China faced major problems that urgently require solutions. The Chinese Government has decided to focus for the coming years on both continuing to improve the economy and also on **making things more equal** for people in China. Wen Jiabao said 'We must always remember that developing the economy is inseparable from improving people's well-being and safeguarding social fairness and justice.'

Wen Jiabao

Top Tip

Although there are huge inequalities in China, the Government has taken a serious approach to reducing these inequalities.

China's 12th Five-year Plan (2011–2015)

We should not only make the cake of social wealth as big as possible, but also distribute the cake in a fair way and let everyone enjoy the fruits of reform and opening up.

Premier Wen Jiabao, February 2011

The Chinese Government introduced a new five year plan in 2011 which focuses on 'higher quality' economic growth. According to President Hu Jintao, an important feature of the new plan is the concept of 'inclusive growth', as China attempts to solve the issue of increasing wealth disparity. The major aims are:

- GDP to grow by 7 percent annually on average
- more than 45 million jobs to be created in urban areas
- population to be no larger than 1·39 billion
- life span per person to increase by one year
- pension schemes to cover all rural residents and 357 million urban residents
- construction and renovation of 36 million apartments for low-income families
- minimum wage to increase by no less than 13 percent on average each year
- improved democracy and legal system.

Wealth

The Chinese Government provides a minimum living allowance of 15 Yuan (£1·10) a month in urban areas and 10 Yuan (73p) in rural areas to 58 million people on low incomes. A total of 60% of these people are in rural areas. The Government also tries to address the unequal wealth situation between the rich and the poor through tax reform. The income level at which people start paying tax was increased in 2008, which means people on lower incomes do not have to pay as much tax as they did previously. The very rich have to pay a very high proportion of tax (45% of their income).

Education and Health

Education

The **Revised Compulsory Education Law**, introduced in 2006, guarantees children free education. China's compulsory education consists of six years of primary school and three years of junior high school. The law stipulates free tuition for compulsory education.

In addition to free tuition, China pledged in 2007 to exempt all rural students from incidental fees to reduce farmers' burdens. It also offered free textbooks and subsidised boarding fees for poor students.

A one-fee system was introduced to stop schools from collecting fees without the Government's knowledge. To fund these policies, the amount of public educational funds allocated for primary education increased from 75% in 1995 to 87% in 2006. The enrollment rate of primary school students increased from 74·6% in 1990 to 99·9% in 2007.

Wealth

In 2002, the Government launched the New Rural Co-operative Medical Care System. This healthcare system was introduced by the Chinese Government in an attempt to make healthcare an affordable reality for the rural poor population in China. Through the Rural Co-operative Medical Care System the cost of medical care is shared by the individual person and the Government; the cost of healthcare is 50 yuan (£5) per person per year. Of that, 20 yuan (£2) is paid in by the central government, 20 yuan (£2) by the provincial government and a contribution of 10 yuan (£1) is made by the patient. The Government aims to provide healthcare to 90% of the population by the end of 2012 and plans to further extend this affordable healthcare system to 100% of the population by 2020.

Employment

The Government has launched numerous initiatives designed to reduce unemployment. **Vocational training** and **entrepreneurship** are the two ways the Government has tried to **reduce mass unemployment**. The Ministry of Education stated in 2008 that vocational schools would enrol 8·6 million new students. Also, several provinces pledged to expand their training institutes. Sichuan made $11 million (US$) in training vouchers available, and Guangxi allocated $35 million to the cause of providing free training to migrant workers. Some provinces have started programmes aimed at inspiring migrant workers to start their own enterprises.

Tackling crime and corruption

The Government tackles crime using **Strike Hard Campaigns**, where it targets particular crimes or regions and gives them harsh sentences. In June 2010 the Ministry of Public Security announced a seven-month strike hard campaign on a number of crimes to curb the rising crime rates. Known in Chinese as *yanda*, the campaign is targeting extreme violent crime, gun and gang crime, telecom fraud, human trafficking, robbery, prostitution, gambling and drugs.

The Government has also acted against corruption. In 2007 the head of the State Food and Drugs Administration, Zheng Xiaoyu, was sentenced to death for taking bribes.

Quick Test 30

1. Outline the main aims of the Chinese Government's 12th Five Year Plan.
2. Describe ways in which the Chinese Government is aiming to reduce wealth inequalities.
3. Describe the measures the Chinese Government has introduced to reduce health inequalities.
4. What initiatives are being introduced to reduce unemployment in China?
5. Explain why Strike Hard campaigns may reduce crime rates.

Political issues: representation

Communist Party of China

China is ruled and organised by one political party – **the Communist Party of China** (CPC). Only the views of the Communist Party count in the decision making of the Chinese Government. The party chairman **Hu Jintao** is the President (Head of State) and has overall control of the Government and China.

Hu Jintao

The CPC claims to have 78 million members; the majority of these members are males over the age of 35. Females and younger adults are under-represented in the CPC.

In order to join the CPC, a citizen must be recommended by two party members, be thoroughly checked and tested by the local party and have a year of probationary membership. Thirteen million new members have joined the CPC in the past decade. Many of these new members will have joined the party to gain access to people who can help advance their careers.

The CPC has local organisations throughout China. Every five years these organisations send delegates to the **National Party Congress**, where they then choose a **Central Committee**. The main job of the Central Committee is to choose a **Politburo** of top party leaders who run the party and the country. It also chooses a **Discipline Commission** to deal with party members suspected of corruption or not following the party line.

The Politburo sets policies and is composed of the top people in the CPC. It is a Cabinet of 24 people, who are secretaries from the big cities such as Beijing and Shanghai, and provinces such as Guangdong.

The real power lies within the **Standing Committee** of the Government. This has nine members from the CPC who hold top posts within the party and government. Members of the Standing Committee include the President, Hu Jintao; the Premier (Prime Minister), Wen Jiabao; and the Chairman of the National People's Congress, Wu Bangguo.

National People's Congress

The **National People's Congress** (NPC) is China's parliament. It meets once a year and is made up of 3000 delegates elected every five years by **Local People's Congresses** in the cities, provinces and armed forces. The real influence lies within the **Standing Committee of the NPC** which has 150 members and meets every two months. The Standing Committee has powers to make laws and change the Constitution. However, as the majority of the members are senior office holders within the CPC, it rarely uses these powers and merely rubber stamps decisions made by the CPC.

Top Tip

Many people join the CPC to enhance their career prospects; it's not what you know, but who you know that is important in the CPU.

The NPC also elects the President and members of the **State Council** and the chairman of the **Military Affairs Commission**. The Military Affairs Commission decides on all matters to do with the **People's Liberation Army**.

State Council

The State Council has 50 members, made up of the Premier, Vice Premiers, State Councillors and the Heads of Ministries. It ensures that Party policy gets implemented and maintains law and order. It draws up the national economic plans and the budget. The full council meets once a month, but a more important **Standing Committee of the State Council** meets twice a week.

Political structure

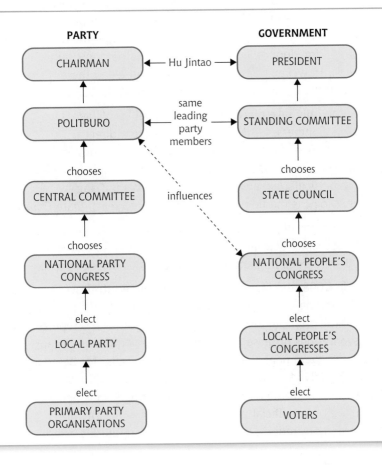

Quick Test 31

1. Describe how the CPC and the Chinese Government are linked.
2. Explain why there is not equal representation in China.
3. Explain the roles of the National People's Congress and the State Council in China.

Political issues: participation

The Chinese Constitution

The Chinese Constitution outlines the structure of the government of China and guarantees the fundamental rights of every Chinese citizen. Rights that appear in the Constitution include the right to vote, the right to stand for election, freedom of speech, freedom of the press, freedom of assembly, freedom of demonstration and freedom of religious belief. However, the people of China can enjoy these freedoms and rights only within the limits laid down by the Communist Party.

Top Tip

Political participation is allowed in China as long as it is within the limits laid down by the CPC.

Opportunities for direct election only take place at the local level for Village Committees and Local People's Congresses. All other elections are indirect within the layers of government. The vast majority of government deputies and ministers are CPC members; however, non-party members can sometimes be allowed to stand if they have particular expertise. For example, Wang Gang, Minister of Science and Technology, is the first non-CPC member to reach State Council level.

The Hukou permit system can restrict migrant workers' participation in local politics. The Shanghai People's Congress did not admit migrant worker delegates until January 2006, and then only as observers, not full representatives. Only in 2008 were three migrant workers selected as delegates to the National People's Congress.

During the Beijing Olympics in 2008, the Chinese Government aimed to show the world that it allows political participation by its citizens by setting up three pre-designated protest parks in Beijing. In order to protest at these parks people had to submit applications to do so. Chinese authorities reportedly received 77 applications to stage demonstrations. Seventy-four of these applications were withdrawn because their grievances were addressed through appropriate government channels, two were rejected for being incomplete and the final application was denied for allegedly violating Chinese law. According to the US-based organisation, Human Rights in China, two elderly Chinese women (79 and 77 years of age) were sentenced to one year of labour for applying to demonstrate in one of the official protest zones. During the Olympics, a small number of foreigners held impromptu, small-scale demonstrations; these individuals were quickly arrested and ultimately deported.

Emerging middle class

Due to the economic reforms there is an emerging middle class in China. These wealthy non-party members are in contact with the West and can see how western business people can influence governments. Since 2007 the CPC, knowing how much economic and social influence rich businessmen have, has been instating more and more private entrepreneurs and professionals as Delegates to the National Congress.

Outside influences

Top Tip

Western influence is coming into China through the internet. However, the internet is policed and censored in China.

China has 420 million internet users, more than any other country in the world. The internet is giving people in China the opportunity to access information that might undermine the party line and because of this the CPC regulates and censors the internet, banning websites if it thinks the content is unsuitable. (This system has been nicknamed The Great Firewall of China.) Examples of sites that are or have been blocked are Amnesty International's website, the BBC news site and MySpace.

Political parties

China is sometimes described as a one-party state. Although there are eight other political parties (known as democratic parties), they are not an opposition to the CPC. They report to the United Front Department of the CPC, share the CPC's aims and rely on its support to get their members into positions of power. No other parties are allowed to operate legally and there is a highly effective state security apparatus to deal with organised dissent.

BALLOT PAPER – POLITICAL PARTIES IN CHINA THE MAIN PARTY	VOTE BY PLACING AN "X"
The **Communist Party of China (CPC):** nearly 80 million members. The founding and main ruling party of the People's Republic of China.	
The eight other legally recognised political parties that take their lead from, and follow the orders of, the CPC	
The **China Democratic League:** 214 000 members, mainly middle class Socialist intellectuals. The party provides a 'third way' between the Nationalists and the Communists.	
The **China Democratic National Construction Association:** 90 000 members, mainly entrepreneurs in the commercial and industrial industries who are Market Socialists.	
Chinese Revolutionary Committee of the Koumintang: Over 80 000 members, mainly left-wing Chinese Nationalists. It is seen by the CPC as the 'second best' political party in China.	
The **Jiusan Society:** 80 000 members, mostly Socialist high level intellectuals in the field of science, technology and medicine.	
The **China Association for Promoting Democracy:** 65 000 members who are mainly intellectuals striving for a Social Democracy.	
The **Chinese Peasants' and Workers' Democratic Party:** 65 000 members, mainly workers from public health, culture, education, science and technology.	
The **Zhi Gong Dang of China:** 20 000 members from a Socialist background. In 2007 Wan Gang, Deputy Chair of the Zhi Gong Party Central Committee, was appointed Technology Minister of the People's Republic of China. This was the first non-Communist Party ministerial appointment in China since the 1950s.	
The **Taiwan Democratic Self-Government League:** 1600 members, mainly Taiwanese Communists who now reside in mainland China.	

Quick Test 32

1. Explain how the rights outlined in the Chinese Constitution are restricted.
2. Describe ways in which people can participate in China.
3. Explain why the emerging middle class is likely to have a big influence on the government in the future.
4. Give reasons both for and against the view that the internet provides freedom of expression in China.

Human rights

'Citizens of the People's Republic of China enjoy freedom of speech, of the press, of assembly or association, of procession and of demonstration.'

Chinese Constitution – Article 35

Workers Statue at Tiananmen Square, Beijing

In spite of the article above, China has received widespread criticism from around the world for its poor record on human rights. Groups such as Amnesty International and Human Rights Watch continually highlight abuses of human rights in China. In the run up to the Beijing Olympics in 2008, some US politicians wanted to boycott the Olympics because of the repressive nature of the government in China.

The Hokou permit system was introduced by the Chinese Government as a way of monitoring the Chinese population. The Hokou permit can restrict a person's access to social benefits such as education and healthcare if they are residing outside of their home town. However, in recent years the Hokou permit has been relaxed in some towns and cities in China. In addition to the Hokou, the Chinese Government holds and records a file detailing a person's life from school onwards called the Dang'an. The Public Security Bureau (PSB) holds the Dang'an and this document can impact a person's right to employment, housing, social security and passport. If someone is suspected of subversion, police and officials have the right to see a Hokou permit or record information on the Dang'an. The State Subversion Laws cover everything from organising and scheming to acting to split the nation, riot or subvert the state. People accused of subversion can be put in jail or even executed. Some of the leaders involved in the Tiananmen Square protests of 1989 are still in jail today.

Migrant workers

Like their parents, children of migrant workers are also deprived of access to many social services. Children in China are entitled to nine years of free education (six years of primary and three years of junior secondary education). However, as cities do not have a responsibility to provide education to children without local Hukou permits, migrant workers' children living in cities need to pay higher fees in order to receive a proper education. This makes many migrant parents leave their children behind in their home towns and prevents many migrant children going on to further education.

Freedom of expression

All means of communication – telephones, mobile phones, faxes, emails, text messages – are monitored in China. The Government has access to the internet service providers and wireless providers operating in China, and has publicly declared that it regularly monitors private email and internet browsing though co-operation with them. The Government also employs several thousand individuals to police the internet. '**The Great Firewall of China**' blocks internet websites of religious, dissent and opposition groups. Foreign news sites are regularly blocked. Bloggers are subject to particular scrutiny in China where such activity is usually not permitted and blogs are, as a general rule, blocked. Access to blogs was, however, relaxed during the Olympics.

Top Tip

Human rights are improving in China. However, the rights contained in the Chinese Constitution are not always upheld in practice.

Religious freedom

'Citizens of the People's Republic of China enjoy freedom of religious belief.'

Chinese Constitution – Article 36

The CPC is suspicious of religions and advocates atheism. It considers Buddhism in Tibet and Islam in Xinjiang to be particular threats. China officially recognises five religions – Buddhism, Taoism, Islam, Catholicism and Protestantism and these religious groups have to register with the State Administration for Religious Affairs (SARA).

Freedom of the person

The Chinese Communist legal system is very different from the legal system that we are familiar with. A person accused of a crime in China may not automatically have the right to have someone represent them; for example, they may not be able to speak to or see a lawyer. The Chinese legal system is more lenient to people who admit their crime, even if they are believed to be innocent. The Chinese police are not obligated to inform an accused criminal of the evidence against them and can refuse to allow an accused criminal to speak in their own defence. China has the highest death penalty rate in the world; it executes more people each year than all other countries in the world combined. The death penalty can be used as a punishment for over 60 crimes, including theft, tax fraud and drug offences. The death penalty can be administered lethal injection, but is more commonly a shot in the back of the head. Families of criminals receiving the death penalty often have to pay for the bullets in order to demonstrate that they understand and accept the reasons for the execution of their loved one.

People can also be sentenced to Laogai (reform through labour). These people face harsh conditions doing very dangerous jobs. People can also be sent to Laojiao (re-education through labour camp) or psychiatric hospitals, often without a trial or predetermined sentence.

Buddhism in Tibet

The Dalai Lama is the spiritual leader of Tibet, which was once an independent Buddhist country. It has been ruled by China since 1951. In 1959 the Dalai Lama fled to exile in India for fear of religious persecution. Since then the Chinese Government has offered incentives to ethnic Chinese to move into Tibet. Ethnic Tibetans are now outnumbered by Chinese by two to one. There have been worldwide protests calling for Tibet to be freed from Chinese rule. According to the group Human Rights Watch, Tibetans are not allowed to enjoy freedom of religious belief. Many Tibetans practising or expressing certain key aspects of their religious beliefs can face coercion, violent repression and imprisonment.

Tibetan flag

The Tibetan flag is banned in China because the CPC believes that the use of the flag indicates the existence of a separate country.

International issues

Falun Gong

The Falun Gong is a spiritualist religious group that blends Taoism, Buddhism and Quigong exercises. In 1999, Falun Gong was declared an 'evil cult' by the CPC, and it is now totally banned. The CPC claims it is a threat to state security. According to Amnesty International, the use of torture, imprisonment without trial and 're-education-through-labour camps' (laogai), have been used against Chinese citizens caught practising Falun Gong. Amnesty International estimates that over 800 Falun Gong followers have been beaten or tortured to death in police custody since 1999. There are reports that the internal organs of some victims had been removed before their bodies were returned to their families.

Gender equality

'Women in the People's Republic of China enjoy equal rights with men.'

Chinese Constitution – Article 48

Traditionally, in China, women are considered less important than men. However, due to a change in employment law, this attitude is changing and women are beginning to be seen as equals in employment and in pay. Despite this, however, women on average earn only 77% of men's pay in China.

Women and girls face human rights abuses due to the **One-child Policy**. Families that have more than one child face fines and social stigmatism. Some families hide births from the authorities but in doing so have limited access to education and healthcare. This has also led to inequality as wealthier families can more easily afford the fines, education and healthcare associated with having more children. Some familes choose to abort female babies and male births now outnumber female births. The one-child policy has resulted in human rights abuses such as forced abortions and sterilisations of women. The CPC intends to continue with the policy in an attempt to curb the growing population. However, it has relaxed the policy for many farming communities and for second marriages where one partner is childless.

Female migrant workers face further human rights inequalities. The harsh working and living conditions of migrant workers put pregnant women at higher risk. In Guangdong, the mortality rate of pregnant migrant workers was 40 per 100 000 persons, compared with only 20 in the general population (China Labour Bulletin 2008). The average mortality rate of pregnant women in developed countries is about 10 per 100 000.

Quick Test 33

1. Describe how migrant workers have fewer human rights than other Chinese citizens.
2. In what way is freedom of expression limited in China?
3. Describe the CPC's view on religion with reference to Tibet and the Falun Gong.
4. Give reasons both for and against the view that the human rights situation for women is improving in China.
5. Explain why the legal system in China could be accused of abusing human rights.

Political structure

To prepare for the exam you should know about the following:
- **The USA political system**
  - The role and powers of the USA Government at Federal, state and local levels.

- **Political issues**
  - Participation and representation.
  - Immigration.
  - Political parties and support from different groups.
  - Political trends.

- **Social and economic issues**
  - Case study: ethnic minorities.
  - The nature and extent of social and economic inequalities.
  - Demands for social and economic change, e.g. in healthcare.
  - The effectiveness of government responses and the consequences for different groups.

Federal system of government

The Government of the USA is based on the **US Constitution**, which was written in 1787. The USA is a union of 50 states. (Every state has its own government, known as the **State Assembly**.) The **Federal Government** is made up of three branches; **the executive (President), the legislature (Congress) and the judiciary (Supreme Court)**. The US Constitution describes what the Federal Government is allowed to do. The powers of the Federal Government include:
- settling disputes between states to prevent them going to war
- taking charge of the military, e.g. the withdrawal of troops from Iraq
- being responsible for international affairs, e.g. diplomatic and trade relationships with China.

Any powers not outlined in the Constitution are reserved for the states and the people. The system of government is set out in the US Constitution. The table below shows how the American people are represented in Congress.

REPRESENTATION OF THE AMERICAN PEOPLE		
The Congress is made up of two chambers …	**The Senate** (Upper house)	**The House of Representatives** (Lower house)
Representatives in each chamber are …	**100 Senators** **2 per state**	**435 members based on the population of the state** California most populated state – 53 members Wyoming least populated state – 1 member

The President

The President is the Head of State and is elected every four years. The powers of the President are set out in the Constitution. His or her powers include:
- The power of appointment
- Commander-in-Chief of the military
- Executive power
- Legislative power

Top Tip

President Obama is the **first ever African American President**. The **ethnic minority vote** was important to his victory, with **95% of black voters voting for him**.

The Powers of the President

	THE PRESIDENT	THE US CONGRESS
Power of Appointment	The President the power to appoint: • **Supreme Court Justices** • **US Ambassadors** • **Other key officials,** for example the head of the Central Intelligence Agency	Each Presidential appointment must have the agreement and approval of the Senate.
Commander-in-Chief of the US military	The President's responsibilities are: • **Defending the USA** from all threats, for instance terrorism • **Protect US interests** around the world. The President's powers include: • **Ordering the use of troops abroad,** for example at the end of 2011 Obama ordered that 17 000 more troops be sent to Afghanistan. • **Agreeing and signing treaties with other countries.** An example would be in 2010 when America and Russia signed a treaty to reduce the number of nuclear weapons they each possessed.	The President requires the approval of Congress to declare war on another country. In 2002 the Senate and the House of Representatives voted overwhelmingly to support the Iraq war. Treaties with other countries have to be approved by the Senate. For example, the Senate voted to approve a South Korea-United States Free Trade Agreement.
Executive power	Executive power means the President has the power and responsibility to: • **Implement laws passed by the US Congress** • **Appoint Secretaries of State** to run Government departments • An example of a Secretary of State is Hillary Clinton, who, at the time of writing, is responsible for foreign affairs.	The US Congress is responsible for passing laws. For example, the Congress passed the Healthy, Hunger Free Kids Act 2010. This law funded free school meals for the next five years and set out nutritional standards for school meals.

Legislative power	The President can only **propose a Bill** (a law); it must be submitted by a member of Congress.
	If the President supports a Bill, he will sign it and it will become law.
	However the President might disagree with the Bill and use his veto.
	Every January the President gives the **State of Union Address** to Congress. This speech outlines:
	• The President's administration's achievements in the past year
	• His plans for the year ahead, including new laws
	• In the 2011 Address Obama announced a number of things, for example:
	  • Ending tax cuts for the richest 2% in America
	  • Education reform
	  • Signing trade deals with Brazil and Chile.
		Once a Bill is submitted to Congress, it is debated and voted on. If the Congress supports the Bill, it is sent to the President to be signed.
		The Bill is returned to Congress, along with reasons why the President vetoed it. **The Congress can overturn a Presidential veto with a two-thirds majority in both Houses of Congress.**

Presidential power under Obama and Bush

The President is the **most powerful person in the USA.** However, each President has a different approach and attitude to using this power.

President Obama (2008–current) and former President Bush (2000–2008) had extremely different views on how to deal with terrorism. After the 9/11 terrorist attacks President Bush issued an **Executive Order** to set up the **Department of Homeland Security (DHS)**. The DHS expanded the powers of the US Government to allow the use of intelligence and surveillance to monitor US citizens as part of the War on Terror. However, Obama disagrees with this and has said that the only time US citizens should be monitored is when they have been identified as a threat to US security.

Another Executive Order enacted by Bush was to grant the **US Attorney General** the power to overturn court decisions on the release of people if it is believed that the person in custody is linked to terrorism. Again, Obama has a very different approach and publicly said he will only use necessary 'legal means' to protect and defend US interests. Obama has also argued that the expansion of Presidential power by Bush was **unconstitutional and therefore illegal under the US Constitution**.

The separation of powers

One of the key features of the US Constitution is the **separation of powers**. This means that each part of the Government – **the legislature, the executive and the judiciary** – is separate from the others.

FUNCTION	PERSON/INSTITUTION	ROLE
Legislative	The US **Congress** – the Senate and the House of Representatives.	**The power to make laws** – a Bill becomes law if it is passed by a majority in both Houses.
Executive	The **President** – appoints Secretaries to run departments, e.g. Defence and Education.	**The power to carry out the laws.**
Judicial	The **Supreme Court** – made up of nine Supreme Court Justices (judges).	**The power to decide what the laws mean.**

The System of Checks and Balances

The US Constitution has **a system of checks and balances** to ensure that no branch of the Government becomes too powerful. The diagram on page 103 shows how this works.

Top Tip

The **US Congress is powerful** and **Presidents have to invest a great deal of time convincing members to support new laws**. For example, President Obama had to persuade a lot of members to vote for health reform. The vote was very close in Congress, with 219 votes for and 212 votes against.

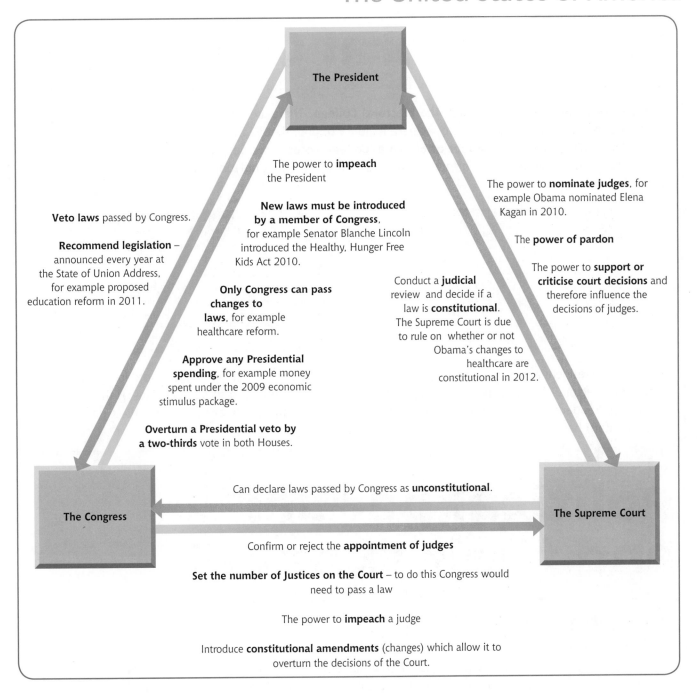

The President

The power to **impeach** the President

The power to **nominate judges**, for example Obama nominated Elena Kagan in 2010.

Veto laws passed by Congress.

New laws must be introduced by a member of Congress, for example Senator Blanche Lincoln introduced the Healthy, Hunger Free Kids Act 2010.

The **power of pardon**

Recommend legislation – announced every year at the State of Union Address, for example proposed education reform in 2011.

Only Congress can pass changes to laws, for example healthcare reform.

Conduct a **judicial** review and decide if a law is **constitutional**. The Supreme Court is due to rule on whether or not Obama's changes to healthcare are constitutional in 2012.

The power to **support or criticise court decisions** and therefore influence the decisions of judges.

Approve any Presidential spending, for example money spent under the 2009 economic stimulus package.

Overturn a Presidential veto by a two-thirds vote in both Houses.

Can declare laws passed by Congress as **unconstitutional**.

The Congress

The Supreme Court

Confirm or reject the **appointment of judges**

Set the number of Justices on the Court – to do this Congress would need to pass a law

The power to **impeach** a judge

Introduce **constitutional amendments** (changes) which allow it to overturn the decisions of the Court.

Quick Test 34

1. What are the key powers of the US President?

2. What evidence is there that President Obama and former President Bush have different attitudes to Presidential power?

3. How do the US Congress and the Supreme Court limit Presidential power?

4. How does the President use his position and power to influence the US Congress and the Supreme Court?

The Electoral College

The US President is elected through the Electoral College. There are 578 Electoral College votes – to become President a candidate needs to secure a majority of one, that is, 270 Electoral College votes. Each of the 50 states has a **different number of Electoral College votes** – two Senators plus the number of members of the House of Representatives. This means that states with a large population have more Electoral College votes than smaller states.

STATE	THE SENATE	THE HOUSE OF REPRESENTATIVES	ELECTORAL COLLEGE VOTES
California	2 Senators	53 members	55
New York	2 Senators	27 members	29
Hawaii	2 Senators	2 members	4
Alaska	2 Senators	1 member	3

Throughout Presidential election campaigns the candidates tend to focus on winning the vote in states with more Electoral College votes, for example Florida. Florida, according to some politicians, is the key to becoming President. In the last four elections (1996, 2000, 2004 and 2008) each President elect (Obama, Bush, Clinton) has secured all the Electoral College votes of Florida.

Political parties and their support

The Democratic Party

President Obama organised a highly successful election campaign in 2008 with a catchy tagline, **'Yes, We Can!'** The effectiveness of the campaign is linked to mobilising key Democratic voters, that is, **women, ethnic minorities and the lowest income groups. Across all groups, Democratic support increased;** the female vote increased to 55% (51% in 2004), the black vote to 95% (88% in 2004) and the Hispanic vote to 67% (53% in 2004).

Democrat party symbol

Supporters were key to the campaign by **providing finance and canvassing voters**. Nearly half of all donations to Obama's campaign were less than $200. These numerous donations added up, and over $500 million was spent on Obama's campaign, compared to less than $400 million by the Republican candidate, John McCain. Obama's supporters helped in many different ways, for example telephone canvassing, holding campaign dinners and driving people to the polling stations. This helped ensure the Democrats won **battleground states,** such as Florida.

Top Tip

The support for the Democratic Party usually comes from **ethnic minorities, women** and **lower income groups**. The success of Obama's campaign in 2008 was in convincing more people to become politically active, for example donating money, canvassing and turning out to vote.

Obama's campaign team in 2008 used the media to great effect. This allowed Obama to broadcast the **liberal** message of the Democrats on TV and the internet. His campaign team used the internet very successfully; over 2 million people supported Obama on Facebook, while only 600 000 supported McCain. Many of Obama's keynote speeches were posted on YouTube and attracted a lot of attention, for example his speech on race was viewed nearly 7 million times on YouTube.

The party is considered to have **more progressive social attitudes** than the Republican Party, such as supporting gay marriage and promoting greater equality, for example increasing taxation on people earning $200 000 a year or more. On foreign policy issues Obama restated his commitment to end the Iraq war, to close Guantanamo Bay and to stop the use of torture on suspected terrorists. These policies tend to be supported in **larger states** and **cities,** such as **Los Angeles** and **New York**.

The Republican Party

Republican party symbol

The Republican Presidential candidate in 2008 was John McCain, who was linked to supporting key policies of President George W. Bush (2000–2008). This association did not help McCain as Bush had one of the lowest approval ratings since the 1930s (25%) by the time he left office. This meant that the Republicans could only depend on their traditional supporters, **the Christian Right and white people**. In 2008 over 70% of the Christian Right voted for John McCain. The results showed that the Republicans won the vote of nearly 60% of white male voters and approximately 40% of white females. It is important to note that traditionally more white women vote for the Republican Party than the Democrats, for example in 2004 55% did so.

Despite the defeat in 2008 the Republican Party has experienced resurgence with **the Tea Party movement**. This resulted in higher Republican voter turnout in the 2010 mid-term elections – over three quarters compared to less than 60% for Democrat voters. The impact was that the Democrats narrowly held onto control of the Senate but their support in the House of Representatives collapsed. The Democrats suffered their biggest drop in support since the 1930s. The main people to benefit were Tea Party backed Republicans, such as **Rand Paul,** a Republican Senator for Kentucky. Nearly half of all Republicans elected to Congress in 2010 had links to the Tea Party. The front person of the Tea Party movement in the Republican Party was **Sarah Palin**. Another key figure is **Michele Bachmann,** who set up the Tea Party Caucus in Congress.

Mainstream Republicans would consider themselves **economically and socially conservative** – this means they **support lower taxation** and support **strong family values,** for instance, opposing gay marriage. The views of the Tea Party supporters are considered ultra-conservative, for example continuing tax cuts for the richest, strong immigration controls and repealing Obama's healthcare reform.

Top Tip

The Republican Party is predominately supported by those in the **Christian Right** and **whites**. The party tends to favour **low taxes for the rich and lower government spending**. It is likely that the **influence of the Tea Party movement will be important in the 2012 Presidential election** and result in more right-wing policies.

Quick Test 35

1. Describe the differences in support for the Democratic Party and Republican Party.
2. Explain why the Tea Party movement is likely to be an important force in US politics in the future.
3. Describe why President Obama's election victory can be linked to being able to mobilise supporters.

Voting behaviour of ethnic minorities

Ethnic minorities comprise approximately **one-third of the US population**. Both parties, the Democrats and Republicans, recognise the importance of the ethnic minority vote and are keen to win their support.

The political influence of African Americans

The Presidential election of 2008 resulted in Barack Obama, America's first African-American President, being elected into office. However, despite this historic event, African Americans still tend to be **less involved in politics than other groups**.

Securing the black vote

The Republicans have tried to secure the support of a range of black groups, such as the black middle class and black churches. Many blacks have conservative views on issues like abortion and gay marriage; for example over 60% of blacks supported Proposition 8, a ban on gay marriage in California. This could suggest that blacks are more likely to support the Republican Party's conservative social attitudes. When in office, President Bush appointed a number of African Americans, for example Dr Condoleezza Rice as Secretary of State.

The biggest challenge the Democrats have faced in recent elections is getting black people to vote. There was an increase in black participation at the 2008 election, with over 65% turning out to vote and 95% voting for Obama. Despite having an African American President in the White House, the number of black voters declined in the 2010 mid-term elections.

Black voter turnout

The 2008 Presidential election was the **first time that voter turnout was similar for blacks and whites**, 65% and 66% respectively. Traditionally blacks have a lower turnout, for example in 2004 only 60% of blacks voted compared to 67% of whites. This trend re-emerged in 2010 when fewer blacks voted than whites.

There are three main reasons why black voter turnout is lower. The first reason is that the black population tends to be **concentrated in areas where the result is easily predicted,** i.e. an area where a black Democrat will win. The impact is that many blacks do not vote. The second reason is that **people who do not graduate school are less likely to vote,** and school dropout rates are high amongst blacks. Again, the consequence is a lower voter turnout amongst blacks. The third reason is the belief that the justice system discriminates against them through **felony disenfranchisement** in states such as Florida and Iowa. This means people are not allowed to vote if they have been in prison. As more blacks are imprisoned than whites, it discriminates against blacks.

The Influence of the Black Caucus in Congress

The **Black Caucus is 43 members (42 Democrats, 1 Republican) in the House of Representatives who promote the interests of African Americans**. At the time of writing, they are campaigning for federal unemployment support to be continued because blacks have a higher unemployment rate.

- After the election of Obama it was believed the influence of the group would increase. However, the relationship has been marked with tension – for instance, the Caucus claims more needs to be done to reduce black unemployment but has had little support from Obama.
- Republican President Bush worked with the Black Caucus in return for their support on other important issues. However, as with Obama, there was some tension in the relationship.
- They **possess approximately 20% of the votes needed to pass a Bill in the House of Representatives**, giving them **considerable influence**. This means House members will support them on black issues in return for votes on other matters.

Lack of representation at the Federal level

Although there is currently a black President, African Americans as a group are still failing to make it into the top level of politics in great numbers.

* Senate – **no black Senators**. Until the 2010 mid-term elections there was one, Roland Burris.
* House of Representatives – **44 members** or 10% of the seats. Blacks comprise 13% of the total US population, so this means **they are slightly under-represented**.

The political influence of Hispanics

Hispanics are under-represented in US politics. Although they are the second largest ethnic group they tend to be **less involved in politics and under-represented**.

Securing the Hispanic vote

Hispanics are the fastest growing group in the USA so their vote is important to both the Democrats and Republicans. The Democrats have tried to win their support with policies that help poorer Hispanics. The Republicans have concentrated on business laws and on demonstrating the party's commitment to strong family values to appeal to the many Hispanics who are Catholic and/or have family businesses.

The Republican Party introduced new laws that allow illegal immigrants to get legal status and eventually citizenship. They also began party political broadcasts in Spanish which were more successful in 2004 (45% of the Hispanic vote) than in 2008 (31% of the Hispanic vote). Former President Bush recognised the importance of the Hispanic vote and he appointed several Hispanics to powerful positions, for example Alberto Gonzales as Attorney General in 2005. President Obama has continued this trend, appointing Hispanics to key posts, such as Sonia Sotomayor to the Supreme Court.

The Hispanic population is **concentrated in a number of swing states: California, Florida and New York**. The Democrats successfully won the Hispanic vote in 2008 with 67% voting for Obama. This vote is significant, for example over 70% of Hispanics in California voted for Obama in 2008, a state with 53 Electoral College votes.

Hispanic voter registration and turnout

The Hispanic vote has become more important in recent elections despite the fact that Hispanics have **one of the lowest rates of voter turnout** of all ethnic groups. The Hispanic vote has become more important as it is concentrated in a number of swing states, for example Florida.

There are over 50 million Hispanics in the USA but around a quarter are not US citizens and are not eligible vote. The **key issue for Hispanic voters is immigration** with nearly 80% rating it as 'extremely important' or 'very important' in the 2008 Presidential election. Despite such a high rate of concern **only 59% of Hispanics eligible to vote registered to do so in 2008,** a minor increase of 1% from 2004.

Lack of representation at the Federal level

The increasing importance of the Hispanic votes means President Obama has appointed a number of Hispanics to high profile positions in the Government and agencies, for instance Alejandro Mayorkas as the Director of US Citizenship and Immigration Services. However, Hispanics are still **grossly under-represented in Congress**.

Quick Test 36

1. Why are ethnic minorities under-represented in the political system?
2. Describe the importance of the Black Caucus in the US Congress.
3. Give examples of how both parties have tried to gain support from ethnic minorities.
4. Explain why the Hispanic vote has become more important.

The immigration debate

Reasons for immigration

There are **nearly 40 million immigrants** in the USA with approximately **25% being illegal immigrants**. There are three key reasons why people immigrate to the country:

- **The American Dream** – the belief that if that you work hard you will be successful.
- **Capitalism** – the USA is the richest country in the world and many people have a very high standard of living.
- **Democracy** – the rights of people are protected by the Constitution. Many immigrants have moved because of war, corruption and oppression.

Arguments for and against immigration

FOR	AGAINST
Employers want **cheap labour** and immigration helps **keep prices low**, e.g. a lot of immigrants work in agriculture.	Wage levels for the poorly paid are **kept low** because there is more competition for poorly-paid jobs.
Immigrants are **young and economically active**. It is estimated that they contribute around $30 billion per year to the economy.	Immigration is **costing the taxpayer a lot of money**. For example, it is estimated that $30 billion is spent on health, education and welfare payments.
According to research by Harvard University, **immigration reduces crime** because immigrants want to stay in the country and to live in good neighbourhoods.	The **US State Department** in 2008 identified Mexican gangs as the biggest organised crime threat to the country. This can be interpreted as **'immigrants cause crime'**.
Cultural diversity is enhanced by immigrants, e.g. greater variety of food.	It is believed by some that **'American' culture is being overwhelmed**. For example 45 million people speak Spanish and there are many Spanish TV channels.
Immigrants bring new skills and **create new jobs**. (This is particularly true of Asians.)	When the economy is in decline some people complain that **jobs are taken by immigrants**.

Attitudes to immigration in Congress

Immigration is a hot political issue in the USA: within Congress, two groups of representatives offer very different views. The **Reclaim American Jobs Caucus** has **41 members in the US Congress** and has a **negative view of immigration**. They argue that there are 15 million American citizens unemployed but there are eight million illegal immigrants working in 'American jobs'.

However, the **Hispanic Caucus** has **23 members** in Congress and **has a positive view of immigration**. This group supports immigration reform, such as the **Comprehensive Immigration Reform Act 2010**. This group believes that millions of illegal immigrants are exploited by employers who do not want to pay tax. Under the Act, immigrants will have to register with the US Government, pay taxes and learn English but will be protected from exploitation.

Interest groups

The issue of immigration has mobilised many US citizens to **protest and join interest groups**.

In 2006, pro-immigration groups organised a protest, **The Day Without Immigrants**. Legal – and some illegal – immigrants did not report for work to highlight the important contribution made by immigrants throughout the USA. The protests occurred in over 50 cities and showed that Hispanics from countries such as Cuba and Mexico are willing to act together to demonstrate that they are important to the US economy.

An important anti-immigration group is the **Minutemen**. It is very active in states bordering Mexico, such as Arizona and Texas, and has volunteers who patrol the border to prevent illegal immigrants coming into the country. They claim their focus is illegal immigration, that they are supported by all ethnic groups and that they act within the law.

Federal and state responses to immigration

Due to the credit crunch and increased Government action at Federal and state level, the number of legal and illegal immigrants has declined. Illegal immigration dropped from 12·5 million in 2007 to 11·1 million in 2009.

Former President Bush introduced a number of new laws and policies to deal with immigration. The **USA PATRIOT ACT** and the **Border Security Act**, both introduced in 2001, restricted and controlled the entry of immigrants into the USA. In addition, a border wall between the USA and Mexico was expanded and the number of **Border Patrol agents** reached a record high of 16 500. Bush also started mission **Operation Jumpstart**, a project to prevent illegal immigrants from getting into the country. This mission provided military support to Border Patrol agents. In 2008, it was estimated that it helped stop nearly 200 000 illegal immigrants from entering into the country but, due to costs, Congress refused President Bush's request to continue to fund it.

President Obama has continued some policies introduced by President Bush. For example, he **increased the number of Border Patrol agents** by 1500 in 2010. The **Comprehensive Immigration Reform Act 2010** has increased funding for security at ports and improved the training of staff so that the rights of immigrants are protected. Furthermore, the Act ensures that states will not be allowed to discriminate against people based on their immigration status.

Obama said, when elected, that he wanted Democrats and Republicans to work together to find a solution to immigration to the USA. Despite this aim, there has been conflict between the Federal Government and some state governments. A number of states bordering Mexico, such as Arizona and California, have expressed concerns over illegal immigration and have taken action, such as **making bilingual education illegal**. The Governor of Arizona, Jan Brewer, criticised the lack of action taken by Obama's administration on immigration. **In 2010, the state passed a law allowing the police to query the immigration status of anyone they stop** and allowing the state to close businesses that hire illegal immigrants. Hispanics have said this will unfairly target them. President Obama has challenged this law in a Federal court; it ruled that Arizona did not have the right to pass this law. However, a recent US Supreme Court ruling stated, 'Arizona has taken the route least likely to cause tension with federal law.' This means that, despite President Obama's views on immigration, the Arizona law is legal and does not breach the US Constitution.

Quick Test 37

1. What are the arguments in favour of and against immigration to the USA?
2. Give examples of action taken by two opposing immigration interest groups.
3. Give examples of attempts to control immigration at both Federal and state level.
4. Describe two key groups in Congress concerned with immigration.

Social and economic inequality

Poverty

Poverty is a significant issue in the USA. According to a recent study nearly 60% of all Americans will spend at least one year in poverty between the ages of 25 to 75. The **rate of poverty has increased consistently since 2007**. The main reason that poverty reached a **record high of 15·3%** in 2010 is the **credit crunch**.

POVERTY RATES BY ETHNIC GROUP					
Year	Total poverty	African American	Asian American	Hispanic	White
2010	15·3%	27·4%	12·1%	26·6%	9·9%
2009	14·3%	25·8%	12·1%	25·3%	9·4%

Source: US Census Bureau

There are distinct reasons why blacks and Hispanics are more likely to live in poverty. Long-term discrimination has created a **black underclass**. Blacks in poverty tend to be single parent female-headed households/dependent on welfare/high school dropouts/long-term unemployed/repeat criminal offenders. Hispanics are likely to live in poverty as many migrate to the USA in search of work and take jobs with very low pay. However, they are more upwardly mobile and many set up businesses, which helps them work their way out of poverty. First generation Hispanics suffer higher levels of poverty when compared to the second and third generation.

Top Tip

The welfare system offers little support and expects citizens to look after themselves. **More blacks depend on welfare.** Therefore, they are more likely to live in poverty.

Unemployment

Unemployment reached a record level of **nearly 10%** in 2010. However, at the time of writing it has shown a decline, and at the end of 2011 had dropped to under 9%. It is unlikely to decline further in 2012 as two thirds of the biggest companies do not intend to hire more staff in 2012.

African Americans face the biggest challenge – unemployment in this group is at a **25 year high with 16% not in work.** This can partly be linked to lower levels of educational attainment but also discrimination by some employers. The impact is that **blacks are more likely to depend on welfare,** Temporary Assistance for Needy Families (TANF), than other ethnic groups.

Hispanics, like blacks, are more likely to drop out of school. However, they do have lower levels of unemployment (currently over 11%). This is because they often work

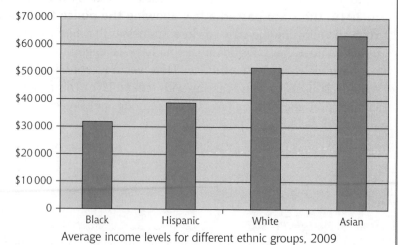

Average income levels for different ethnic groups, 2009

in family businesses, such as restaurants, or become self-employed. **Asian Americans and whites have the lowest levels of unemployment,** at 6·4% and 7·6% respectively. This is because they have a higher proportion of high school and college graduates than the other ethnic groups.

Education

Asian and white Americans tend to do well in the US educational system because they often live in areas with good schools and can afford to pay for higher education. However, **blacks and Hispanics** tend to do less well according to a report by the National Association for the Advancement of Colored People (NAACP). Problems with schools include poor quality of school facilities, lack of materials such as textbooks and limited course choices.

Former President Bush introduced the **No Child Left Behind Act** in 2001, although it was not funded sufficiently for it to be effective.

YEAR	TOTAL DROPOUT RATE	HISPANIC	BLACK	WHITE
2000	13%	27·8%	13·1%	6·9%
2005	11%	22·4%	10·4%	6%
2010	8%	18%	10%	5%

Source: Child Trends Databank

In 2009, President Obama introduced the **Race to the Top** program. This provided additional funding of $4 billion in grants to help lower-performing schools and to deal with high dropout rates. **Every year around 1.2 million American children do not graduate from high school.** The **College Opportunity and Affordability Act (2008)** doubled grants available to students and increased funding for colleges for low income and minority students.

There is a clear link between level of education and income and unemployment.

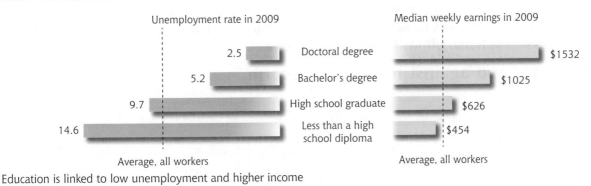

Unemployment rate in 2009 / Median weekly earnings in 2009

	Unemployment	Earnings
Doctoral degree	2.5	$1532
Bachelor's degree	5.2	$1025
High school graduate	9.7	$626
Less than a high school diploma	14.6	$454

Average, all workers

Education is linked to low unemployment and higher income

Health

The issue of healthcare has proved to be controversial in the USA. Unlike the UK, there is no state-funded health service like the NHS. Under President Bush the number of Americans with **no access to healthcare reached 46 million**, and during the Presidential election campaign in 2008 Obama promised to introduce healthcare reform.

The reality is that many people have to pay for private health insurance; but often it is provided via employers. **Blacks and Hispanics experience higher levels of unemployment and are therefore less likely to be able to afford healthcare**. They depend on basic healthcare that is provided through Medicaid or Medicare.

Top Tip

Regularly check US Government sites and news websites **to examine the impact of healthcare reform in the USA**.

International issues

Due to a number of factors, blacks and Hispanics have **lower life expectancies**. Firstly, the leading cause of death for young black males is homicide. For young Hispanic males it is the second leading cause of death. Secondly, both have high rates of HIV/AIDS. (50% of all cases are in the black community and 20% of cases are in the Hispanic community.) Thirdly, they have higher rates of obesity and associated health conditions such as diabetes and strokes.

The table below highlights lack of health insurance and resulting inequalities by ethnic group.

HEALTH INDICATOR	BLACK	HISPANIC	WHITE	ASIAN
No health insurance	21%	32·4%	12%	17·2%
Life expectancy	Male: 70 Female: 75	Male: 77 Female: 82	Male: 75 Female: 80	Male: 80 Female: 85
Infant mortality rate	13·3	5·5	5·6	4·6

Healthcare reform

Healthcare reform has proven to be a heated political issue in the USA. Obama's reforms aim to ensure that an **additional 32 million people will have access to healthcare**. When healthcare reform was debated in the US Congress it **was mainly Republicans who opposed it**, often claiming that it would become more expensive and bureaucratic. However, Democrats who supported reform pointed out that the USA already has **one of the most expensive healthcare systems in the world**. The debate has mobilised public opinion with interest groups such as **Physicians for a National Health Program (PNHP)** campaigning for healthcare reform and others such as **Hands off My Health** opposing reform.

Arguments for and against healthcare reform

FOR	AGAINST
The majority of Americans believe healthcare is a right. For example, a survey in 2009 showed that 64% agreed that it is a right.	The healthcare provided would be decided by the Government and not insurance companies. This means **people will have fewer choices**.
According to research, **poor healthcare coverage is expensive;** it is estimated to cost between $65 and $130 billion each year.	**Government spending would have to be increased significantly;** by 2020 it is estimated that the US Government would be spending another $593 billion to fund healthcare.
Healthcare is **crucial to the functioning of society** and should be guaranteed for all Americans.	Healthcare reform is allowing the Government **greater control and healthcare should not be an area in which the Government has influence**.
Healthcare reform will save money. It is estimated that for every dollar spent on healthcare, 31 cents go to insurance companies. Full healthcare coverage could save $400 billion per year.	**Healthcare reform will not save money.** Administrative costs for the Government-funded health programme will be the same as for private health insurance (13·2%).

Housing

Access to quality housing is linked to income; as blacks and Hispanics have, on average, lower income, many live in **ghettos** (slum areas, containing mostly minorities) and **barrios** (poor areas occupied mostly by Hispanics) in the inner city. **Low income** and **discrimination** have made it difficult for them to get mortgages. For example, it is twice as difficult for blacks to get mortgages than it is for whites. An example of discrimination would be **redlining**, which is the practice of mortgage lenders drawing red lines around parts of cities where they do not offer loans – these are mainly in black areas. Access to mortgages has reduced due to the **credit crunch**, affecting blacks more than any other group. The following table shows the effect of the credit crunch on housing ownership.

YEAR	BLACK	HISPANIC	WHITE	ASIAN
2004	49·1%	48·1%	72·8%	59·8%
2009	46·2%	48·4%	71·4%	59·3%

Social housing in Chicago

It is estimated that **9·3 million Americans live in poor quality housing** in ghettos, such as some areas of the Bronx in New York City. Features of ghettos include high unemployment, high crime rates and lack of access to facilities, such as shops and play parks.

One way for city authorities to deal with these problems is through higher spending. Inner city areas have lower tax revenue because of **white flight and black middle class flight** – this means people move to the suburbs. The lack of tax revenue means it is difficult for cities to invest and improve inner city housing conditions. Segregation is a feature of housing in the USA, with whites tending to live in all-white suburbs, and blacks and Hispanics living in areas predominately populated by others from the same ethnic groups.

Top Tip

A lot of Americans do not like 'big Government' and argue that it restricts freedom. For example, they do not think the Government should provide healthcare. The issue of healthcare is likely to remain a controversial issue in American society.

Crime and justice

Blacks and Hispanics are **more likely to be involved in crime** than other ethnic groups because crime is concentrated in inner cities. The main reasons blacks and Hispanics are involved in crime are high unemployment, family breakdown, street gangs and drugs. Due to the high levels of poverty, the money that can be made from crime is attractive to the young unemployed.

Families play important roles in determining whether young people become involved in crime; for example over 80% of black families are lone-parent families, but the majority of Hispanics are supported by strong extended families. Their lack of strong family units means that more young black males are likely to turn to crime, while Hispanics are likely to become involved in the family business.

Blacks and Hispanics are likely to face inequality in terms of justice. For example, research in California has found that, when sentenced for similar crimes, Hispanics receive 6·5 months longer and blacks 1·5 months longer than whites. Furthermore, blacks are four times more likely than whites to be in prison, and two-and-a-half times more likely than Hispanics. In 2009 the majority of prison inmates were either black or Hispanic. For example, 39% of prisoners were black despite the fact that only 13% of the population is black. Hispanics are also over-represented in the prison population, with 20% of prisoners having Hispanic backgrounds despite the fact only 15% of the US population is Hispanic.

Why inequalities continue

Economic reasons

There are three main economic reasons why social and economic inequalities continue in the USA: 'White Flight', 'Black Flight' and reductions in welfare spending.

White Flight has negative impacts on inner cities as many white people who have jobs and pay tax have moved to the suburbs. The consequence is that these people no longer pay tax in the inner cities. This means that there is less money available to fund essential services such as schools.

The growth of the black middle class has also presented challenges, mainly because of **Black Flight**. This means that when blacks become better educated and have higher-paying jobs they, along with whites, move out of inner cities to the suburbs. The impact is that, within the ghetto, there is **a lack of positive role models**. This means that young black males, in particular, may turn to criminal activities such as gang violence and drug dealing to fund their lifestyles.

Unlike the UK, the US Government has a very limited programme of welfare to support its poorest people. The main form of support that is provided is **Temporary Assistance for Needy Families** (TANF). When TANF was introduced in 1996, over 12 million households received payments. However, due to changes in the rules, by **2010 only 4·4 million households were entitled to TANF.** TANF payments have not increased at the same rate as inflation, meaning that the poorest people in American society **have less money** for essentials like food and rent. The lower welfare payments have **hit minorities hard as they represent 65% of all families receiving TANF**; 40% are black and 25% are Hispanic. Following the recession, the Federal Government made an additional $5 billion available for TANF payments between 2009 and 2010.

Social reasons

The economic crisis of 2008 has led to **cuts in services** that are important in helping people move out of poverty, such as education. The lack of funding for schools, particularly inner city schools, means young people become **disengaged with education**. The lack of **good role models** in the community means some turn to crime, for example many young black boys are brought up without a father. Those that do complete high school and go on to university are likely to **face discrimination in the job market**. These challenges mean blacks and Hispanics are more likely to be trapped in a **'Vicious Cycle of Poverty'** from which they find it difficult to escape.

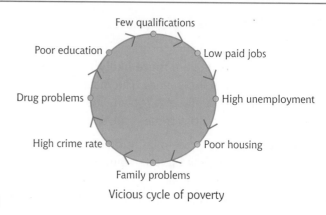

Few qualifications

Poor education

Low paid jobs

Drug problems

High unemployment

High crime rate

Poor housing

Family problems

Vicious cycle of poverty

Political reasons

Despite the election of the first ever African American President, many ethnic minorities remain **disillusioned** with the political system. Although Obama depended on the support of blacks and Hispanics in the 2008 Presidential election, many did not vote for the Democrats in the 2010 mid-term elections. This is mainly because many ethnic minorities are unhappy about high unemployment rates and the lack of government help.

Obama has attempted to deal with the social and economic problems faced by the people of the USA, but this has proved particularly challenging. In April 2011 the Federal Government was one hour away from shutting down as the Democrats and Republicans could not agree government spending for 2011 to 2012. After much tense negotiation, an agreement was reached between President Obama and the Republicans in which Federal Government spending would be reduced by $39 billion.

The issue of Federal Government spending is likely to remain a sensitive political issue with the **growth of new political movements such as the Tea Party**. They have argued for massive reductions to welfare schemes such as TANF. The Tea Party movement has also campaigned against the healthcare reforms introduced by Obama. Their supporters believe that healthcare is the responsibility of individuals and that the Government should not be intervening in private healthcare. Supporters of the Tea Party movement also feel that welfare, healthcare and education should not be available to illegal immigrants.

Top Tip

Many ethnic minorities believe President Obama is not doing enough to help them despite the introduction of free healthcare. However groups such as the Tea Party believe the role of the Government is expanding too far and costing too much money.

Quick Test 38

1. Describe the impact poverty has on the living standards of ethnic minorities.
2. Explain why education is a positive route out of poverty for ethnic minorities.
3. Explain why African Americans are more likely to experience social and economic inequalities.
4. Describe the health inequalities suffered by at least two ethnic minorities.
5. Why do social and economic inequalities continue?

Answers

Devolved decision making in Scotland

Quick Test 1

1. The founding principles of the Scottish Parliament are accessibility, accountability, the sharing of power and equal opportunities.
2. Devolution is where a central government passes limited powers to a regional government.
3. Some powers are reserved to the UK Parliament because Scotland is not an independent state (country) and so that matters affecting all of the UK are handled the same way across the UK.

Quick Test 2

1. AMS is a hybrid system of First Past the Post and the Party List system. The electorate votes for a constituency MSP and also a party. There are 73 constituency MSPs and 56 list MSPs in the Scottish Parliament.
2. Advantages include voters being able to 'split their tickets' and give their support to smaller parties. The percentage of votes a party secures reflects the seats it ends up with. Disadvantages include AMS not being wholly proportional as it favours the large parties. Some voters find the system confusing. At the 2007 election, there were 140 000 invalid ballot papers.

Quick Test 3

1. It could be argued that coalitions lead to more democratic government because the wishes of more people are taken into consideration, while encouraging parties to co-operate and share power rather than engage in confrontational politics. On the other hand, no-one votes for a coalition government, and small parties can end up with a disproportionate amount of power effectively becoming the 'king maker'.
2. Minority government can work in Scotland – this was demonstrated during the 2007–11 session. The SNP had to rely on other parties to pass laws. However, there were many manifesto points which the SNP were unable to pass – a good example being the inability to cancel the Edinburgh tram project.

Quick Test 4

1. MSPs can submit oral or written questions to Scottish Government Ministers. They can put forward a question for FMQs, held every Thursday. (Questions for FMQs are selected by the Presiding Officer.) MSPs can also consider the views of their constituents while making decisions in the Parliament's committee meetings.
2. Committees act as checks and balances on the powers of the Parliament. They can propose laws. The petitions committee must consider all petitions submitted to it. The Scottish Parliament committees convene outside Edinburgh – taking the Parliament to the people of Scotland.

Quick Test 5

1. To a great extent – a great deal of day-to-day work is carried out by civil servants despite politicians in Westminster and Holyrood arguing.
2. The Calman Commission was led by Sir Kenneth Calman. It was supported by all main parties apart from the SNP. The commission recommended the transfer of powers to Scotland surrounding air weapons, Scotland being given control over drink-drive limits and the power to change speed limits on roads. It also recommended that powers of insolvency, charity law and registration of health professionals be returned to Westminster.

Quick Test 6

1. The Barnett Formula is the method used to calculate changes in the amounts of money allocated to Holyrood by Westminster for devolved areas. Changes in the amounts allocated to England are reflected in the amounts allocated to Scotland, after taking into account how comparable Scottish and English areas of spending are and the relative sizes of the populations. However, once calculated, the money allocated to Scotland can be spent however the Scottish Government wishes.
2. The SNP believes Scotland should be independent and they see the money which Scotland receives from Westminster as 'pocket money'. At the time of writing Scotland does not have control over funding and does not raise its own taxes.

Quick Test 7

1. STV was introduced as part of the coalition agreement of 2003 between the Liberal Democrats and Scottish Labour. It was a Liberal Democrat demand for going into coalition.

2. Councils being reluctant to support ASBOs is an example of conflict. The freeze on council tax has also seen great strains placed on the relationship between the Scottish Government and Scotland's councils. The Trump development in Aberdeenshire is a very high-profile example of conflict.

Decision making in Central Government

Quick test 8

1. The Prime Minister has a variety of powers as head of the Executive. Different Prime Ministers have used the powers of the office in different ways. The Prime Minister is leader of his or her political party as well as being head of the country and the main representative of the UK in foreign affairs and negotiations. He or she is also an MP and must represent constituents. Among other powers, the PM has the right to 'hire and fire' members of the Cabinet, make appointments to the Church of England and play a role in the honours system (awarding MBEs, etc.).

2. Prime Ministers are limited in power in a variety of ways. They are always looking to have public opinion on their side particularly in the lead up to elections. Sometimes Cabinet colleagues can resign or threaten to resign over certain issues, which can limit the freedom of action a PM enjoys. James Purnell is an example of a high profile resignation from Gordon Brown's Cabinet. A hostile media can also weaken a PM. Gordon Brown was attacked by newspapers like the *Daily Mail* and the *Sun* and had a consistently negative public image among large sections of the electorate.

3. The Cabinet must discuss major issues before Government can act. Ministers have an input into policy. Sometimes Cabinets can force a Prime Minister to change course. However, a PM exerts great influence over Cabinet, setting their agenda and summing up their mood. Ministers must also publically support the decisions of the Cabinet as a whole as long as they remain Ministers.

Sometimes Prime Ministers will attempt to bypass Cabinet and rely more on the advice of special advisors.

4. Special advisors are different from civil servants because they are not permanent staff and will be loyal to their Minister and his or her political party. Civil servants are permanent staff and must give impartial advice and implement policy regardless of the party in power. Civil servants and special advisors might even give conflicting advice to Ministers due to the different perspectives that they have of Government.

Quick Test 9

1. The function of the House of Commons is to represent the people of the UK. Each MP is elected to speak for and advance the interests of the people of a geographical constituency and to 'call Government to account'. It must vote on proposed legislation, called bills, most of which are introduced by the responsible Government Minister. The House of Commons is also the branch of Parliament that has the say over Government spending. Parliament votes on the Government's budget every year though, in practice, a Government with a clear majority will have little opposition to its budget. Another important function is to allow debate between Government and Opposition. It also provides the MPs who form the Government.

2. The Opposition is the second largest political party in the House of Commons. It is the job of the Opposition to challenge the Government. The Opposition must present itself as a credible alternative to the current Government. Opposition MPs act as 'shadows' to Ministers and the Leader of the Opposition will have the opportunity to ask the PM questions every Wednesday at 12pm.

3. It is one of the main jobs of MPs to hold the Government to account. They can do this by debating important issues or proposed legislation, asking questions at Prime Minister's Question Time or questions of individual Ministers, and through work on committees. These are small committes of MPs which examine a specific aspect of the work of the Government. These Select Committees may take evidence from experts, call the Minister and civil servants for questioning, and publish recommendations. The House of Lords can also amend or return Government Bills though not financial Bills and, under the Salisbury Convention, should not vote against the second or third reading of a Bill which is in the Government's manifesto.

4. The most significant difference between the House of Lords and the House of Commons is that the House of Lords is unelected. The Lords is a second 'revising' chamber which can only delay or suggest changes to Bills which are not related to the Government's budget.

Quick Test 10

1. Pressure groups are organisations which are dedicated to a particular cause or goal. Although the law is decided in Parliament, pressure groups provide individuals with a way of making their voice heard when decisions are being made. At the same time, pressure groups do not seek power through the electoral system and are therefore different from political parties. They also campaign on a narrow range of issues or even a single issue.

2. Pressure groups fall into different categories. There are **cause groups** and **interest groups**. Cause groups campaign on issues and attract members and supporters who feel passionate about a particular cause. Stop the War Coalition is an example of a cause group. Interest groups, on the other hand, represent the interests of their members. The Educational Institute of Scotland is an example.

3. Pressure groups use a variety of methods to influence those in power. Peaceful campaigns such as protest marches and lobbying may elicit more public sympathy. But more radical members may become frustrated if these tactics do not appear to be working. The protest against the Iraq war in 2003 brought millions out to demonstrate but ultimately failed to prevent the war. Pressure groups may therefore turn to more violent or illegal direct action. Publicity stunts or law breaking may, however, attract media attention but fail to gain public sympathy.

4. Pressure groups encourage and provide individuals with an opportunity to shape the decision making process, especially those who feel passionate about a particular cause but do not join political parties. However, the most influence is held by large and well-funded groups and others may be squeezed out, thereby distorting the democratic process.

5. TV, radio, newspapers and the internet are the source of most people's political information. While TV must be neutral, other forms can take sides and provide one sided coverage. Newspapers sometimes take on the role of an unofficial Opposition to the Government, questioning its decisions and exposing wrongdoing, as in the MPs' expenses scandal. At the 2010 election most newspapers supported the Conservative Party. Politicians all seek to use the media to their advantage, such as the party leader TV debates which took place for the first time in Britain in 2010. Despite the impressive performance by Nick Clegg, the increased support that the Liberal Democrats gained from the debates did not turn into votes on election day. The effect that TV debates will have on the outcome of elections should not be overstated. New forms of media have also made an appearance. The popularity of social media such as *Twitter* means that politicians have to be very careful in what they say, as in the case of the Labour candidate who posted obscene comments on *Twitter* during the 2010 election.

Electoral systems, voting and political attitudes

Quick Test 11

1. FPTP discourages people from voting at general elections. Votes are often wasted – especially in safe seats. The use of FPTP can result in negative and/or tactical voting, that is voters giving their votes to candidates they dislike the least.

2. Through comparing the results of the 2010 General Election, it is clear that Labour and the Conservatives do well through the use of FPTP.

3. The 2010 election saw no party secure enough seats to form a government. This seldom happens due to the use of FPTP. FPTP *usually* delivers a majority for one party and *usually* avoids coalition governments. The election result in 2010 was the first time, since February 1974, that there has not been one party with an overall majority.

Quick Test 12

1. MEPs are elected through the Party List System. Voters have no say on the individuals who become their representatives. Voters merely give their support to parties.

2. To a large extent the results of the 2009 European election are far more proportional than the 2010 General Election. At the European election, the Conservatives secured 27·7% of all votes cast and returned 35% of UK MEPs. In comparison, the Conservatives secured 36·1% of the vote at the UK General Election in 2010 but won 47·2% of the seats in the House of Commons.

Answers

3. There is no evidence to suggest that PR leads to increased voter turnout. At the 2009 European elections, only 35·5% of people who were entitled to vote did so.

Quick Test 13
1. Voters have two ballot papers, one to elect their constituency MSP and one to vote for the party of their choice.
2. It was felt that FPTP was too disproportionate. Had FPTP been used to elect MSPs, the Scottish Labour Party would have won 93 out of 129 seats at the Scottish Parliament Election in 1999. The devolved settlement was created to strengthen the UK. Some commentators believed the use of AMS would prevent the SNP from gaining an outright majority.

Quick Test 14
1. Looking at the implementation of STV in Scotland, one negative point is that there is no link between elected representatives and constituents. Depending on which ward they live in, a constituent now has three or four councillors. On the other hand, this can be positive as there is more chance of there being an elected councillor that a constituent voted for.
2. AV is used in the leadership elections for Labour and the Liberal Democrats. It is used in the elections for UK parliamentary officials, including Select Committee Chairs. It is used in membership organisations, businesses and trade unions' internal elections. Most student union elections use AV.
3. A referendum is a ballot of all voters on a new law.
4. Referenda are not held frequently in the UK.
5. 11 September 1997.

Quick Test 15
1. Class dealignment is where traditional class categories begin to unravel and blur. The ways in which voters perceive themselves and the social classes to which they belong change.
2. Labour lost support among the working class due to policies which appealed more to the middle classes.
3. Ed Miliband is concerned that five million votes were lost by Labour between 1997 and 2010. One-third went to the Liberal Democrats, and most of the rest simply stopped voting. Most of this change occurred within the working class population.

Quick Test 16
1. Labour performed very well in Scotland at the 2010 election but lost a lot of seats in the south of England.

2. Caroline Lucas' performance can be seen as a success. She is the first Green Party candidate elected to Westminster.
3. The SNP did not do as well as they expected to. The SNP hoped to find themselves in a position of being 'kingmaker' whereby they could get concessions for Scotland. Their target of twenty seats was not achieved: they only won six.

Quick Test 17
1. The main issues middle class women consider are issues affecting them and their families directly, with education being key.
2. Low levels of voter turnout among the BME community are attributable to feelings of alienation, deprivation and religious intolerance.
3. Political parties are courting the BME vote to secure power. There are many constituencies in the UK where there are many BME voters whose support could be decisive in winning certain seats.

Quick Test 18
1. To a great extent they are ineffective. A survey conducted by Ipsos Mori found that nearly three-quarters (74%) of those polled agreed that paying household bills is preferable to watching party political broadcasts.
2. There is evidence to support this view after the Scottish *Sun* ran with the headline 'Play it again Salm' in the 2011 election, in reference to Alex Salmond.

Social issues in the United Kingdom: wealth and health inequalities

Quick Test 19
1. **Unemployment and low wages** can cause poverty. Unemployment is the absence of a job, meaning that an individual will have to live on benefits. The **Job Seeker's Allowance** is the latest name for unemployment benefit. It is designed to encourage people to find work by only providing enough money for a minimum living standard. The maximum JSA payment for a single person aged 25 or over is £67·50 per week. This is not sufficient to provide a high standard of living, although other benefits are

available even if also claiming JSA. Currently about 2·5 million British people are unemployed. Furthermore, there are only about 0·5 million job vacancies.

Being a lone parent makes an individual more vulnerable to poverty than other types of family. Nearly 90% of lone parents are female making this a gender inequality issue. Furthermore, two-thirds of the 4 million people on low pay are women who are working part time in low skilled jobs. Some of these women will be lone parents, making them and their children vulnerable to poverty.

There is inequality in the tax system. As a proportion of their wealth, the rich pay less than the poor. The current top rate of income tax is 50% for individuals earning £150 000 a year or more. In the 1970s, the top rate was 83%. Since 1979, both Conservative and Labour Governments have cut direct taxation and increased indirect taxation such as VAT.

2. Women and ethnic minorities may suffer from problems, which can limit opportunities for employment and promotion and possibly lead to poverty. Some examples of these problems are:
Pregnancy and career breaks can lead to missed promotion opportunities. Women with university degrees face a 4% loss in lifetime earnings as a result of motherhood, while mothers with no qualifications face a 58% loss. There is also **pay gap between the earnings of men and women.** This is despite the fact that girls from all ethnic groups outperform boys in education.
Racial discrimination may be a reason for high levels of ethnic minority unemployment: in 2010 48% of blacks aged 16–24 were unemployed compared to 20% of whites. In 2010 nearly three-quarters of Bangladeshi children and half of black African children in Britain were growing up in poverty.

3. Overall, Government policies have had a mixed record of success. With regard to racial and gender inequality the record of anti discrimination legislation is mixed. The **Equality Act** has been criticised for promoting **reverse discrimination** of white men while the Government's citizenship tests have become something of a joke. The Conservatives failed in their plans to provide **cash incentives for married couples.** The current Government is attempting to **improve conditions for business** so more jobs are created in the private sector. However, they will also cut hundreds

of thousands of jobs in the public sector. A new medical assessment has been introduced, the Work Capability Assessment. This assesses what a person can do, rather than what they cannot, and then identifies a range of health-related support they will need to return to work as around 7% of adults cannot work due to ill health, and receive benefits such as the ESA. However, anti-poverty charities have claimed this will lead to those who are unfit to work being pushed into jobs. The Labour Government introduced the **National Minimum Wage (NMW)** currently £6·08 if over 21. However, many trade unions still believe the NMW is set too low and have begun a campaign for a far higher 'Living Wage'. The Scottish Labour manifesto in 2011 promised this for the public sector.

4. Two examples of the effects of poverty on everyday life are:
Social exclusion – Individuals and families being unable to play a full part in society, often due to poverty and low income.
Educational underachievement – Children may be sucked into a 'cycle of poverty' where their circumstances lead to low attainment in education, which in turn denies them their clearest route out of poverty and social exclusion.

Quick Test 20

1. If you are poor, you are less likely to be healthy. This link was first established by the Black Report in 1980.
2. Lifestyle choices lead to poor health. For example, around 86% of all lung cancer deaths are caused by smoking. Poor diet leads to problems including diabetes, hypertension, stroke, cardiovascular disease and some cancers. 25% of the population of Scotland are obese.
3. Two other (linked) causes of poor health are geographical location and social class. Statistics show that those in social class AB (for example doctors) have a life expectancy of around seven years more than those in social class DE (for example cleaners).
Geography is linked to social class as some areas have far higher rates of socio-economic deprivation (high unemployment, poor housing, low paid jobs). There is a geographical divide within a number of British cities. Life expectancy in the Glasgow Eastend community of Calton is 54 but in Lenzie (to the north of the city) it is 82. This is linked to inequalities in wealth and class differences – unemployment in Calton is around

Answers

10% compared to 3% in Lenzie, where poverty and low incomes are also rare. The difference in health and life chances between the neighbouring communities of Bearsden and Drumchapel is also marked.

4. **Free personal care for the elderly** has been a popular policy of the Scottish Government. The **Winter Fuel Payment**, to prevent fuel poverty and the health problems arising from poor housing, such as hypothermia and asthma, is also popular but could be seen as a waste of money as all receive regardless of income. The Government has put large sums of money into initiatives such as **Sure Start** and **Healthy Living Centres**.

5. Local Government
   Fuel Zones in schools (Glasgow City Council)
   Scottish Government
   • Free Personal Care
   • Sure Start
   • Healthy Living Centres
   • Transfer of Housing Portfolio to Housing Associations, e.g. GHA
   Central Government
   Winter Fuel Payment

6. There is a relationship between the different causes of poor health. For example, poor lifestyle choices are likely to be made by someone who is poorer and lives in a disadvantaged area of a city. Social classes D and E tend to live in the areas which are overwhelmingly disadvantaged, thus establishing a link between class and geographical location.

Quick Test 21

1. **Individualists** argue that individuals should be left alone to look after themselves. It is no one's fault but the individual's if he or she is poor, fat, or addicted to drugs. Governments should therefore step out of the way and stop taking taxes from hardworking people to fund expensive programmes for the lazy, selfish and indulgent. Welfare programmes in fact discourage people from taking the first step towards a better life by starting on a low paid job and working up. It is therefore actually kinder to cut off these programmes – a policy of 'tough love'. Governments must stop 'nannying' us to quit smoking, drinking alcohol or eating junk food. Individuals are capable of weighing up these choices and making their own decisions.
   Collectivists argue that an individual's circumstances largely dictate their life chances. A child born into a poor family with parents who are drug users is unlikely to study hard at school or pursue an active healthy lifestyle. Poor housing

and crime can also shorten life expectancy and these problems are more prevalent in poorer areas. It is up to Government to use the tax system to redistribute wealth from those who have done well to the poor to ensure a more equal society. Anyone can suffer poor health and unemployment at the same time and it is therefore better to have a social safety net. Cutting off or reducing welfare may catch out cheats but punish their children who are ultimately innocent.

2. Labour represents a more **collectivist** approach while the Conservatives **are more individualist**, although the reality is a lot more complicated.

3. Some individualist thinkers have suggested that people can be **'nudged'** into making better individual choices – e.g. marriage, giving up smoking, working hard, etc. – rather than being lectured to or told what to do by a 'nanny state'. Then Government, rather than lecturing people or stepping out of the way, will create the conditions for people to make the right choices.

4. **Individualist view of private healthcare**
   Individualists have no problem with this as they are suspicious of Government control and believe that individuals should make their own provision for healthcare. Some individualists criticise the fact that everyone must pay for the NHS through taxation regardless of whether they use it or not.

   Collectivist view of private healthcare
   Collectivists would claim that private healthcare promotes inequality: the founding principle of the NHS was that everyone had equal access to treatment regardless of ability to pay and if private health providers became more involved in the NHS, they would 'cherry pick' the richest patients and a 'two tier' system would result – with the oldest, poorest and sickest being left to an overstretched NHS.

   Individualist view of welfare reform
   Some individualist thinkers have argued that Government hand-outs are too generous and encourage people to be lazy and selfish and should therefore be reformed. They would argue that people should be more self-reliant. Hardworking families should not pay taxes for the lazy to sit about all day. They also point to the fact that unemployment has become an intergenerational problem in cities such as Glasgow and Liverpool and that it is in some cases not financially worthwhile to take a job as more money is available on benefits, often supplemented with unofficial earnings on the

'black economy'. Welfare reform would involve drastically cutting benefits to make work more attractive or forcing claimants to undertake some socially useful work, such as gardening or street sweeping. This approach was undertaken in the USA and had the effect of drastically cutting the numbers of welfare recipients.

Collectivist view of welfare reform
Collectivists would point to the 'heartlessness' of welfare reform and claim that it would involve a return to the Victorian **workhouse**, where poor and desperate families were humiliated simply because the main breadwinner had lost his job or died. They also argue that it is not in keeping with the founding principles of the Welfare State, where the Government pledged to look after the most vulnerable members of society 'from the cradle to the grave'. And during a time of high unemployment, it is not clear if there are enough jobs for people who are kicked off welfare. Ultimately, collectivists argue, children would suffer for the failings of their parents and society would see a massive increase in poverty. They therefore reject welfare reform.

South Africa

Quick Test 22
1. Parliament is made up of two houses: the National Assembly and the National Council of the Provinces. The President, who is elected by the National Assembly. The Constitutional Court, the highest court in South Africa.
2. The key powers of the President include appointing the Deputy President and the Cabinet to run the country.
3. The Constitutional Court has 11 judges; they are not allowed to be members of political parties and the Government has to follow the rulings of the court.
4. The national and provincial governments work together on areas such as education, health, housing and welfare.

Quick Test 23
1. South Africa could be said to be a one-party state because the ANC has won every election since 1994, with over 60% of the vote. However, it could also be said that it is not a one-party state because of the growth and increasing importance of other political parties, such as the DA and COPE.
2. The main political opposition is the DA. The DA has highlighted the lack of success of the ANC in government and campaigned to be a non-racial alternative to the ANC.
3. The **ANC** is the biggest and most powerful political party in South Africa. Its main aim is to eradicate the socioeconomic inequalities that are linked to the history of Apartheid. The biggest challenge faced by the party is that of internal divisions.

The **DA** is the second largest political party in South Africa. It has fought election campaigns highlighting the failure of ANC policies and tried to gain support from all ethnic groups in the country.

COPE aims to deal with the problems of crime, poverty and unemployment.

IFP is similar to COPE, but also wants to deal with the AIDS crisis and aims for increased power-sharing between the different levels of government.
4. The role of pressure groups in South African politics is still developing. Pressure groups, such as the Congress of South Africa Trade Unions, have been criticised for being too closely linked to the ANC. It is also believed that the ANC is suspicious of pressure groups that are not loyal to the party.

Quick Test 24
1. Evidence that the ANC has support throughout South Africa is that they are the dominant political party at every level of government and run the majority of the nine provinces in the country.
2. The ANC is the dominant political party because the majority of the black population support the party and it has strong support from the trade union movement.
3. Voter turnout increased in 2009 because of changes to voting laws and because many people are unhappy with the pace of change made by the ANC.
4. For a healthy democracy: range of political parties in the country, political parties share power in one province, decline in support for the ANC.

Against a healthy democracy; ANC has dominated all elections since 1994, strong link to the trade union movement, control eight out of nine provinces.

Quick Test 25

1. Crime is a major problem because of poverty, high levels of unemployment, alcohol and drug abuse, absence of a stable family life.
2. **Access to education**: two-tier system that favours the wealthy; high school fees prevent many children from attending school.

   Access to healthcare: 80% of the population depend on government healthcare, which is underfunded; access to healthcare varies across the country, for example Eastern Cape has greater health problems than Western Cape.
3. HIV/AIDS epidemic with 5·6 million cases; 310 000 died from AIDS in 2009.
4. Lack of educational success means it is difficult for people to find jobs; experiencing unemployment/poverty means they find it difficult to pay for a good education, access quality housing and decent healthcare.

Quick Test 26

1. Workbooks available in all 11 languages, no-fee status of schools, the Teacher Laptop Initiative, Kha Ri Gude campaign.
2. GEAR replaced RDP in order to strengthen the economy by creating jobs, reducing poverty and privatising state assets.
3. Affirmative Action is a form of positive discrimination. Examples include:
   - offering non-whites jobs and promotion opportunities
   - companies having to ensure that their workforce reflects the population.
4. The aim of BEE is to create a more equitable society by having more blacks in senior and middle management positions.

Quick Test 27

1. The impact of the 2010 World Cup included improved infrastructure. 300 000 new jobs were created, resulting in increased economic activity. This was accompanied by 90% drop in crime.
2. The South African Government has introduced a number of policies to help the poorest in the country, for example: no-fee status of schools to help the poorest to access education for their children; introducing free healthcare for pregnant women and children under six; expanding immunisation programmes to improve health; the Housing Subsidy Scheme and Community Residential Units Programme to help deal with high rents; the Framework of the New Economic Growth Path, which aims to create 5 million new jobs.

3. The HIV/AIDS epidemic has had a negative impact upon the social and economic development of the country – it is estimated that there are 850 deaths a day due to the disease. The disease is mainly killing young people, that is, young workers, and so damaging the country's economic growth. Many children are brought up by grandparents.
4. **Education**: progress
   National School Nutrition Programme, Teacher Laptop Initiative, increase in number of no-fee status schools.
   Education: lack of progress
   Concerns remain about the standards of teaching, high school graduation is less than 70%.
   Housing: progress
   Access to water and basic sanitation has improved, Government support for high rents through the Housing Subsidy Scheme, Community Residential Units Programme.
   Housing: lack of progress
   Improvements to housing have been hindered by the HIV/AIDS epidemic, 5 to 15 million people still live in shanty towns, slow progress on land redistribution.
   Health: progress
   Free healthcare is available for pregnant women and children under six, building 3000 new rural clinics, Expanded Programme on Immunisation has increased the number of children vaccinated against preventable diseases.
   Health: lack of progress
   Life expectancy has continued to fall from 61 in 1990 to 49 in 2011, around 15% of children are not still vaccinated against preventable diseases, HIV/AIDS is a serious problem with around 850 deaths per day.

China

Quick Test 28

1. China was traditionally a closed economy whereby the Communist Government owned and controlled all businesses and industries. However, since the 1970s, China has changed the way it runs the economy, closing the inefficient state-owned enterprises, ending the iron rice bowl, and moving to an open-door policy with the rest of the world.

   Millions of Chinese citizens relied on SOEs for employment and social support such as housing and healthcare. However, as a result of their inefficiency, many state-owned enterprises closed down, causing high levels of unemployment and poverty.

2. The Household Responsibility System allowed farmers to grow and sell surplus food on the open market, and removed restrictions on what they were allowed to produce. Rules for industry were also relaxed, allowing factories to produce goods to supply market demand rather than to meet government quotas.

3. SEZs were set up around coastal areas of China to allow goods produced there to be exported easily. Businesses setting up inside SEZs enjoyed tax incentives and cheap labour, encouraging the economy to boom. In 2001, China joined the World Trade Organisation (WTO) which resulted in foreign trade doubling in China and allowed Chinese companies to invest abroad and many more foreign companies to invest in China.

4. With an estimated 100 million rural residents over the last decade leaving the countryside in search of employment in the big cities, it is the largest migration of people in the world. Migrant workers provide cheap labour for both multinational companies and state-owned enterprises in China. Migrant workers, desperate for employment, often work long hours in factories for very little pay.

Quick Test 29

1. In 2010, the annual average per capita disposable income of citizens from rural China was 5900 yuan. This was much less than in urban China, where the average per capita disposable income of citizens was 19 100 yuan.

2. Urban China has 108 billionaires, the second highest number of billionaires per country. (Only the USA has more.)

3. People living outside of their Hukou permit area have to pay more for schooling and healthcare.

4. Although China is a communist country, healthcare is not free for all and there is a great deal of inequality in the Chinese healthcare system. Individuals often have to rely on private medical insurance. Therefore poorer people may not be able to afford decent healthcare. Corruption is also a big problem for the health system: hospitals cannot make much money from the poor, so they often increase prices for richer patients' operations.

    Provision for education is unequal as there are large costs associated with attending school. Families have to pay education fees for books, stationery, uniforms and equipment. This cost increases for those living outside their Hukou

permit areas. The result of these fees is that children of poorer families and migrant worker families are more likely to drop out of school early or are put off attending school.

5. Large-scale unemployment has contributed to the rise in petty crime. Organised crime – counterfeiting, money laundering, theft, kidnapping, human smuggling and drug trafficking – is a growing problem in China. This new trend of organised crime has created a huge hidden economy. The rise in crime rates has been blamed on the breakdown of Mao's Communist ideals of discipline and the rise of capitalist competition, as well as links between the police and criminal gangs.

6. **Better**
    More rich Chinese, better access to western luxuries, opportunity for private enterprise.

    Worse
    Greater inequalities, a huge divide created between the rich and poor, increased crime rates, poor conditions of migrant workers.

Quick Test 30

1. Growing GDP by 7%, creating jobs in urban areas, capping the population at 1.39 billion, increasing the life span of citizens by one year, ensuring that pension schemes cover all rural residents and 157 million urban residents, constructing and renovating 36 million apartments for low-income families, increasing the minimum wage by no less than 13 percent on average each year, improving democracy and the legal system.

2. Tax reforms which mean people on lower incomes do not have to pay as much tax. The very rich have to pay a very high proportion of tax (45% of their income).

3. Rural Co-operative Medical Care System – Government pays for a proportion of medical costs.

4. Vocational training and entrepreneurship. Training vouchers to provide free training to migrant workers.

5. Harsh sentences, including the death penalty, for a variety of crimes.

Quick Test 31

1. China is ruled and organised by one political party – the Communist Party of China (CPC). Only the views of the Communist Party count in the decision making of the Chinese Government.

2. One-party state, CPC members get special treatment and 'benefits' by joining the party.

Answers

3. The National People's Congress (NPC) is China's parliament. It only meets once a year. The NPC also elects the president and members of the State Council and the chairman of the Military Affairs Commission. The State Council has 50 members, made up of the Premier, Vice Premiers, State Councillors and the Heads of Ministries. It makes sure party policy gets implemented and maintains law and order. It draws up the national economic plans and the budget. The full council meets once a month, but a more important Standing Committee of the State Council meets twice a week.

Quick Test 32

1. The people of China can only enjoy these freedoms and rights within the limits laid down by the Communist Party in China. Opportunities for direct election only take place at the local level for Village Committees and Local People's Congress. All other elections are indirect within the layers of government. The Hukou permit system can restrict migrant workers' rights.

2. Rights that appear in the Constitution include the right to vote, stand for election, freedom of speech, of the press, of assembly, of demonstration and of religious belief. However, these rights are heavily restricted.

3. These wealthy non-party members are in contact with the West and can see how western business people can influence governments.

4. The internet provides a window to the world outside China and China has more internet users than any other country in the world. The Chinese Government, however, censor the internet. Many internet sites are blocked.

Quick Test 33

1. Chinese cities do not have a responsibility to provide education to children without local Hukou permits, so the children of migrant workers living in cities need to pay higher fees in order to receive a proper education.

2. All means of communication – telephones, mobile phones, faxes, emails, text messages – are monitored in China. The Government has access to internet service providers and wireless providers operating in China. The Chinese Government has publicly declared that it regularly monitors private emails and internet browsing though co-operation with local internet service providers.

3. The CPC is suspicious of religions and advocates atheism. It considers Buddhism in Tibet to

be a particular threat. Tibetans practising or expressing certain key aspects of their religious beliefs can face coercion, violent repression and imprisonment. In 1999, Falun Gong was declared an 'evil cult' by the CPC, and it is now banned.

4. The change in employment law is positive – women are meant to be paid the same as men. However, the one child policy violates women's rights.

5. The Chinese legal system is more lenient to people who admit their crime, even if they are innocent. China uses the death penalty more than any other country in the world, executing more people each year than all other countries combined. People can also be sentenced to *laogai* (reform through labour) where they are faced with harsh conditions doing very dangerous jobs. They can also be sent to *laojiao*, (re-education through labour camp) or psychiatric hospitals, often without trial or a predetermined sentence.

United States of America

Quick Test 34

1. The key powers of the US President include the power of appointment, legislative power and executive power.

2. President Bush believed that the US Government should increase the use of intelligence and surveillance to reduce the risk of terrorism. President Obama argued that this increase was unconstitutional and stated that he will use only 'legal means' to protect the USA.

3. The US Congress limits the powers of the President by having the power to pass and change laws, approve government spending, and having the ability to overturn a Presidential veto with a two-thirds majority. The Congress can also impeach the President if he is suspected of any wrongdoing. The Supreme Court limits the powers of the President by deciding how the law will be carried out, and the judges have the power to declare decisions or laws to be unconstitutional.

4. The President seeks to influence Congress by getting support for new laws; for example, President Obama invested a lot of time

convincing members of Congress to support the healthcare reform. The President seeks to influence the Supreme Court by appointing judges and by commenting on their decisions.

Quick Test 35

1. The Republican Party's main support is from traditional small-town America and the Christian Right. It favours traditional moral values and is predominantly white in it's make-up.
   The Democratic Party's main support tends to be concentrated in big cities such as New York and support more progressive social values. Key supporters are ethnic minorities, women and lower income groups.

2. The Tea Party movement will be more important in US politics because it has support from a significant number of Republican voters. This support helped the party gain a large number of seats in the House of Representatives in the 2010 mid-term elections. Nearly half of all Republicans elected to Congress in 2010 have links to the Tea Party.

3. President Obama's election victory was linked to mobilising supporters – they donated money to the campaign, phoned people and attended campaign rallies.

Quick Test 36

1. Ethnic minorities are less likely to be involved in politics. For example, blacks and Hispanics are less likely to be registered to vote than whites. In addition, even if they are registered to vote, they are less likely to use their vote.

2. The Black Caucus is important because it has approximately 20% of the vote in the US House of Representatives.

3. The Democrats and Republicans have tried to attract ethnic minorities by having policies that they support. For example the Republicans hope to win part of the black vote by demonstrating the party's strong family values. Another way is through appointing ethnic minorities to important positions, such as Obama's appointment of Sonia Sotomayor to the Supreme Court.

4. The Hispanic vote has become more important because they are the fastest-growing ethnic group in the USA and they are concentrated in a number of swing states such as California, Florida and New York.

Quick Test 37

1. **Arguments for immigration:**
   - cheap labour, immigrants are young and contribute to the economy,
   - reduces crime,
   - increases cultural diversity,
   - brings new jobs to the USA.

   Arguments against immigration:
   - wage levels are kept low,
   - costs a lot of money in education, health and welfare payments,
   - causes crime, overwhelms 'American' culture,
   - jobs are taken by immigrants.

2. The **Day Without Immigrants** highlighted the important contribution made by immigrants to the US economy. The **Minutemen** tried to prevent illegal immigrants from crossing the US-Mexico border.

3. **Federal level:**
   The USA PATRIOT Act, the Border Security Act, Border Patrol agents, Operation Jumpstart and the Comprehensive Immigration Reform Act.

   State level:
   making bilingual education illegal, Arizona law permitting police to query the immigration status of anyone stopped by them.

4. One group is the **Reclaim American Jobs Caucus** which has a negative view of immigration. Its members argue that there are currently 15 million unemployed Americans, while eight million illegal immigrants are working in 'American jobs'.

   Another group is the **Hispanic Caucus** which has a positive view of immigration. It argues that immigrants are exploited by employers who do not want to pay tax or decent wages. It supports reforms such as the **Comprehensive Immigration Reform Act 2010** which enables immigrants to register with the US Government, pay tax and learn English.

Quick Test 38

1. The impact of poverty means that ethnic minorities, particularly African Americans and Hispanics, are less likely to graduate from high school, find suitable employment or afford decent healthcare and are more likely to become involved in gang-and drug-related crime.

2. Education is a positive route out of poverty because it leads to better incomes. For example, in 2009 people with degrees earned on average $1025 per week, while people without high school diplomas earned on average $454 per week.

3. African Americans are more likely to experience social and economic inequalities as they are less likely to do well in education. Lack of education means they find it difficult to find employment. Even if they do get jobs, they are likely to be paid

Answers

less than whites. Many blacks are 'trapped' in the ghetto and lack positive male role models and turn to gang violence and crime.

4. Hispanics are more likely to lack health insurance (32·4%). 21% of blacks have no health insurance. Blacks have the lowest life expectancies of all ethnic groups in the US, at 70 years for males and 75 years for females.

5. Inequalities continue because some groups of people depend on TANF, are caught in the poverty trap and are disillusioned with the political system.